Woodlands

WILDSIDE

Tess Lemmon

Conserving animals and plants in a changing world

BBC BOOKS

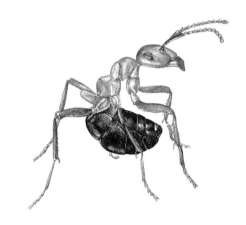

Published by BBC Books,
a division of BBC Enterprises Limited,
Woodlands, 80 Wood Lane, London W12 0TT

First published 1992

ISBN 0 563 36169 7

Designed by Neville Graham

Printed in Great Britain by
Butler & Tanner Ltd, Frome and London

Contents

About this book

IF THE WORLD'S top 10 inventors put their heads together, it might take them a very long time to come up with a machine that could do half the things a tree can do. For a start, they would have to build a gigantic air-freshener that pumped out oxygen all the time. Then they would have to make hundreds of small pieces and fix them in just the right position to trap energy from the sun. And *then* they would have to make the whole thing keep itself going by drawing up water from deep underground.

Put lots of these contraptions together, and you've got a world that contains the perfect conditions for all sorts of animals from bears to bats. A woodland.

Whether it's a small, tangled thicket or a towering wilderness, a woodland is as full of magic and mystery as any tropical rainforest. But, like the rainforests, the woodlands are under threat. Many have already been destroyed, and we need to take action now to protect the ones that are still here.

This book looks at the lives of woodland animals and plants, and at the problems they face. What does a woodpecker do when it's left with no wood to peck? Why is the koala fighting against extinction? It also looks at what people are doing to save the woodlands, and suggests lots of ways in which you can join in.

A woodland world

Good woods

HUMAN BEINGS ARE NOT the only ones who need regular meals and a comfortable bed to sleep in. Animals do too, and woodlands provide plenty of food and homes to suit all shapes and sizes, from a beetle to a bear. Any time of day or night, animals are busy building or improving their nests, dens or burrows. And when it comes to finding food, there's something for everyone. There are greens, nuts, berries and fruits for vegetarians, and anything from tiny insects to large deer can feature on a meateater's menu.

You won't find trees and other plants hurrying about like the animals, but they're just as lively. They're putting down roots, sending up shoots, developing buds, flowers and leaves, creating the woodland world

Above: The seasons set the rhythm of life in a deciduous woodland. Autumn signals the end of one cycle and the beginning of another: the dead leaves will break down on the woodland floor and feed the soil for spring's new growth.

Above left: 'Home sweet home' is a hole in a tree for this pine marten. Mammals, birds, reptiles and insects all use trees as refuges, resting places, and look-out posts.

Left: A caterpillar tucks into its meal. The different parts of a single tree provide food for a whole range of animals from insects to antelope.

Below left: Many woodland flowers appear in early spring, before the leaves of the trees have shaded out the light. Primroses are some of the first to poke up from the ground each year.

Bad woods

SUPPOSING A STRANGER came along and took over your room and stole all your food. Worse, supposing that stranger came along in a bulldozer and flattened your home to the ground. When we destroy woodlands, we're not just killing the trees and other plants, but robbing all the animals of their world. For nearly two million years, ever since the Stone Age, people have been clearing away woodlands to make more room for themselves – but the more space we take up, the less there is left for other living things.

Nor are we very good neighbours to the animals in the woodlands that are still left standing. They are trapped for fur, or hunted for sport, or killed out of fear and dislike.

WILDSIDE WATCH

Whether you live near a woodland or not, there are all sorts of things you can do to protect woods and their wildlife.
● Find out about conservation groups in your neighbourhood.
● Get your hands dirty if necessary: plant trees or turn a piece of waste ground into a nature reserve.
● Persuade people to look after woodlands by telling them about all the wildlife that lives there.

Above: We use wood to make everything from tables and chairs to paper and pencils; but spare a thought for where it all comes from. Cutting down trees destroys the worlds of many plants and animals.
Above right: The face of an outlaw. The wolf has been persecuted for hundreds of years. It has been completely wiped out from many woodlands.
Right: The perils of modern life can reach even the wildest woodland and its wildlife. This sparrowhawk has died from eating prey poisoned by pesticides sprayed on farm crops.
Below right: Hunters hold up their kill. Thousands of woodland animals are shot and trapped for their fur, or meat – or just for sport.

Key trees

TREES CAN GROW almost everywhere on Earth except the polar ice-caps. Wherever they grow a whole world of animals and plants is found on them, in them, and under them. From their hidden root systems to their highest branches, trees support intricate webs of life.

There are many woodland worlds. Each type of woodland is dominated by certain kinds of trees. The thousands of different species of tree belong to two main groups: coniferous and deciduous. Coniferous trees thrive in cold climates. They blanket mountains and cold northern regions. Pine, spruce, fir and larch are all common types of conifer. Flourishing where there is ample summer warmth and rainfall are the deciduous trees that have broad, flat leaves. Oak, ash and beech are all common types.

Coniferous trees

THE ANIMALS AND PLANTS of coniferous woodlands live in a rather dark world. Conifers are known as evergreens because they don't shed their leaves all at the same time. A coniferous forest is therefore always very shady. Some plants, such as heathers and mosses, thrive in these conditions – and a whole range of insects, birds and mammals have ways and means of making a living amongst the straight trunks and needle-like leaves.

Wood lark
Slightly larger than a sparrow, it nests in the lower branches of conifers, where it is well-camouflaged by its dark colours. Two families are raised in spring and summer. The wood lark migrates to northern Africa for winter.

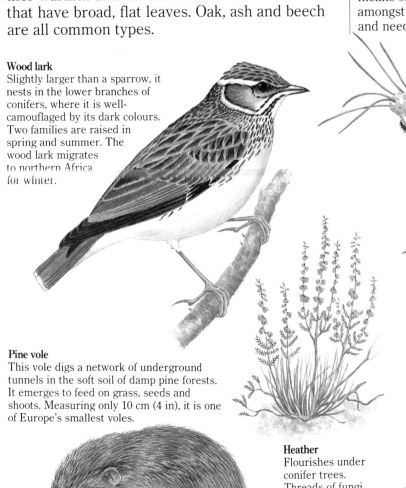

Pine vole
This vole digs a network of underground tunnels in the soft soil of damp pine forests. It emerges to feed on grass, seeds and shoots. Measuring only 10 cm (4 in), it is one of Europe's smallest voles.

Caterpillars of the pine processionary moth
On the branches of pine trees, the caterpillars spin tents of silk and spend the winter inside them. On warm days they come out to eat pine needles, marching in a procession down the tree.

Heather
Flourishes under conifer trees. Threads of fungi living on its roots help it survive in poor soil. Mice and voles hide in tussocks of heather, and eat the seeds.

Deciduous trees

IN DECIDUOUS WOODLANDS, flowers, shrubs and trees grow in distinct layers. Each layer provides a home and food for insects, birds and mammals, and contributes to the diversity of life in the woodland. In winter, deciduous trees go into a dormant state, very much like an animal hibernating, and their leaves die. Even with their broad leaves, deciduous trees are less dark than coniferous ones, so on the woodland floor many flowers are able to bloom early in spring before they are shaded by the canopy.

Caterpillar of the lobster moth
This caterpillar feeds on the leaves of beech, oak, birch and hazel trees. It squirts formic acid at birds which try to eat it. It also threatens them by raising its head, waving its legs about, and bending its swollen rear end over its body – which makes it look a bit like a lobster.

Wood warbler
This bird always nests on the ground. It prefers beechwoods because the undergrowth is not too thick. The wood warbler flies high in the trees, hunting insects. It spends summer in Europe and winter in central Africa.

Bird's nest orchid
Named after its tangled roots which look like a bird's nest, it thrives in the darkest parts of beechwoods because it doesn't need sunshine to help it grow. Instead, it depends on the decaying leaf litter. Unlike most plants, it is not green, but yellowish-brown all over.

Weasel
The smallest carnivore in the world, the weasel measures only about 20 cm (8 in). It hunts voles, rabbits and rats which are often much larger than itself; also climbs trees to eat bird's eggs.

WILDSIDE WATCH

The next time you visit a woodland, look for clues that will help you to identify what sort it is.
- Are there plants that are found only in this type of wood?
- What are the dominant trees?
- Is it generally light or dark?
- What signs of seasonal change are there?
- Are there signs of animals - tracks, or discarded food?

Ancient woodlands

THE FIRST GIANT FERNS to tower over the Earth looked nothing like the pines and oaks of today, but by 200 million years ago there were trees which you would recognise – and dinosaurs walked amongst them. It took many more millions of years before animals like squirrels or cats appeared in the woodlands.

Life on Earth is changing all the time, but it doesn't happen overnight. On the million-year time-scale, people have been here a very short time, during which we have managed to do a lot of damage.

Only a few pieces of ancient woodlands are left, and they give some idea of the past. But we need to look forward too, and make sure all woodlands have a future.

Bison in Bialoweiza

WATCHING A HERD of European bison is like going back in time. Centuries ago, these massive, shaggy-headed animals roamed the forests of Europe and Asia. Today, they seem completely at home in Europe's oldest woodland. As they stand feeding peacefully, it looks as if the modern world has passed them by.

But all is not what it seems. These animals have suffered so much from human activities that by the 1920s they were completely wiped out in the wild. Some died when woodlands were cleared, and others met the same fate as the American bison, and were hunted until none was left. The very last European bison found refuge in an ancient forest in Poland, but was shot in 1919. Soon afterwards, a group of people got together to try to save the species by breeding bison that were in captivity. Now, some herds have been set free, and have become wild. The largest herd is alive and kicking in the same place where the last wild bison died: Bialowieza National Park in Poland.

Below: Close cousin of the European bison is the American bison, or buffalo. Between 40 and 60 million of these animals used to live on the North American plains, but white settlers hunted them to the brink of extinction.
Bottom: European bison, or wisent, in Bialowieza National Park, Poland. The park is one of the last fragments of ancient forest left in Europe. Some parts are untouched by human beings.

Vital statistics

TREES GO ON GROWING all their lives. They not only get taller, but also fatter. They put on weight regularly year by year, and this is marked by a series of rings inside the trunk. Counting the rings on any tree stump will tell you how long a tree was alive. But you don't have to wait for a tree to die before it reveals its age. All you need to do is find out how fat the tree is by measuring round the trunk. And to tell whether the whole woodland is old or new, all you need to do is look around you.

Telling the age of trees

The living tree
To get a rough idea of the age of a living tree, measure right round the trunk, at about 1.5 m (5 ft) from the ground. Then do a quick calculation.
If the tree is growing close to others: 1.25 cm (½ in)=1 year.
If the tree is on its own: 2.05 cm (1 in)=1 year.

Flower power
Flowers give clues about the age of a woodland. Old woodlands usually have more variety than young ones. Some species of flower grow only in ancient woodlands. Identify what you see, and find out what conditions they need.

Tree stump
The inside of a tree is marked by rings. Each ring equals one year's growth – so count them to find out the tree's age when it was cut down.

WILDSIDE WATCH

Many different things – like climate and type of soil – influence how well a tree grows.
● Carry out your own experiment and take a series of measurements from the same type of tree growing in different places: a woodland, a park, a built-up area.
● Keep a record of each tree's growth rate, and suggest reasons for any variations.
● Take a good look at the tree's bark. The outer bark can't stretch as the tree gets fatter, which is why it cracks, peels and flakes. Sometimes you can see old and new bark on the same tree. Bark is very different on different trees, so is a good way of identifying them.

Looking after woodlands

WOODLANDS ARE THE CENTRE of a lot of attention. They are regularly checked over by foresters, and constantly studied by scientists who find out new things about them all the time. These experts use their knowledge to look after woodlands, but not everyone who works with woodlands is on the spot. People in offices also make decisions about a woodland's future.

Then there's us. We can all do our bit to care for woodlands when we visit them. But woodlands can also be ruined by people, and sometimes the best way of looking after them is to keep out.

All over the world, people are protecting woodlands. Conservationists in New South Wales, Australia, try to persuade loggers not to fell trees.

National Park

PLENTY OF TREES flourish in freezing temperatures and deep snow. Across the north of Europe, the USSR, and North America, there are woodlands whose plants and animals have all sorts of ways of coping with the cold. The trees are mostly hardy conifers, and the animals have thick coats or a good covering of feathers.

The wildest woodlands are the coldest and most remote, because no human can easily brave the conditions. But others are being cut into by roads. When the roads end, people take off across the snow and ice on snow-scooters. Slowly, more and more wilderness is being taken over.

Many areas are specially protected. One such place is Sarek National Park in Sweden, where bears and wolves, eagles and elk, all live in safety. But lately, snow-scooter tracks have been showing up, and conservationists are fighting to make sure that the only signs in the snow are the footprints of the animals that belong there.

Above: Snow may look pretty, but it creates harsh conditions for plants and animals to live in. Left: This Siberian jay copes with the bitter cold by puffing up its feathers to trap a warm layer of air between them.

Standing up for trees

IF YOU COULD TAKE 40 men and stack them up on each other's shoulders, the top one would be as high as the tallest tree in the world. It's the giant sequoia, also known as the 'big tree'. Giant sequoias are the largest living things on Earth, and also some of the oldest. They can still be going strong after 3000 years.

These trees and their equally huge cousins, the coast redwoods, used to be a common sight in North America, but most of them have now vanished. Within the last 150 years they have been felled, and their wood turned into everything from houses to pencils. Removing the trees destroys the whole woodland. With almost no plants or animals around them, the very last giants stand alone. People trying to save them have a real battle on their hands. They have resorted to climbing the trees and tying themselves to branches to stop the loggers from cutting them down.

WILDSIDE WATCH

You don't have to be in and around a woodland to look after it!
● Read your local newspaper: woods are sometimes cleared before interested groups and people know what is happening.
● Be prepared. Be up-to-date with local plans for new buildings that may threaten woodlands. Local newspapers and libraries have the information.
● If you come across any threats, let your local conservation groups know.

These giant sequoias are the largest living things. Huge groves of them used to tower over the Earth – but within the last 100 years people have cut down most of them for their wood.

After the storm

SWAYING, CREAKING, and cracking, the sight and sound of a falling tree seems like one of the worst things that could happen in a woodland. But there's more to this than meets the eye. For one thing, trees don't have such a clear-cut division between life and death. Unlike people and animals, they don't simply lie down and stop breathing. Many fallen trees go on living and growing, and many dead trees stay standing up! Also, one part of a tree can be quite dead while another part goes on living.

Then again, dead and dying trees are teeming with life. Hundreds of plants and animals depend on them. And when the wood finally crumbles away, it helps to feed the soil and give life to the next generation. Far from being over and done with, a fallen tree is an essential part of a healthy woodland.

Untidiness rules

FIFTEEN MILLION TREES blew down in one night when a hurricane hit Great Britain in 1987. People quickly cleared up all the mess. The fallen trees were chopped up and taken away, and soon everything was neat and tidy again. But sometimes clearing up can do more harm than good. Of course, trees that block roads or smash into buildings must be removed, and some half-broken ones may be about to land on someone's head – but what about the ones lying in the woods?

To get to them, tractors rip their way through the forested area, churning up the ground and disturbing the wildlife. Many fallen trees are still alive, but meet their deaths when chainsaws slice them up. Taking them from the woodland deprives plants and animals of food and homes. Fallen trees are full of life: inside, outside, underneath, everywhere you look. Fungus sprouts from them, and moss grows all over them. They are literally crawling with insects which thrive on mouthfuls of wood, and they are regarded as highly desirable places to live. Snakes, salamanders and mice are just some animals that like nothing better than a hole in a mouldy log.

It seems that fallen trees are breaking the rules by showing us that being tidy isn't *always* a good idea!

Fallen trees provide us with a good stock of firewood. But are we too hasty? With only one-sixth of its roots in the soil, a fallen tree can survive and send up shoots. Some trees can be uprighted and fitted back into their holes in the ground.

Breaking and entering
Over 1000 species of animals and plants live on rotting wood! The first residents break into the newly fallen tree, and open it up for everyone else.

Longhorn beetle larvae
These larvae hatch from eggs laid under the bark by the female beetle which bores through the hard wood. Larvae eat wood.

Sulphur tuft fungus

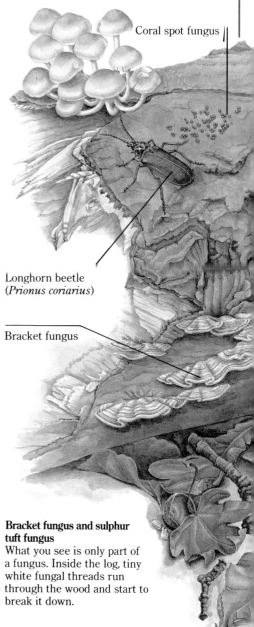

Coral spot fungus

Longhorn beetle (*Prionus coriarius*)

Bracket fungus

Bracket fungus and sulphur tuft fungus
What you see is only part of a fungus. Inside the log, tiny white fungal threads run through the wood and start to break it down.

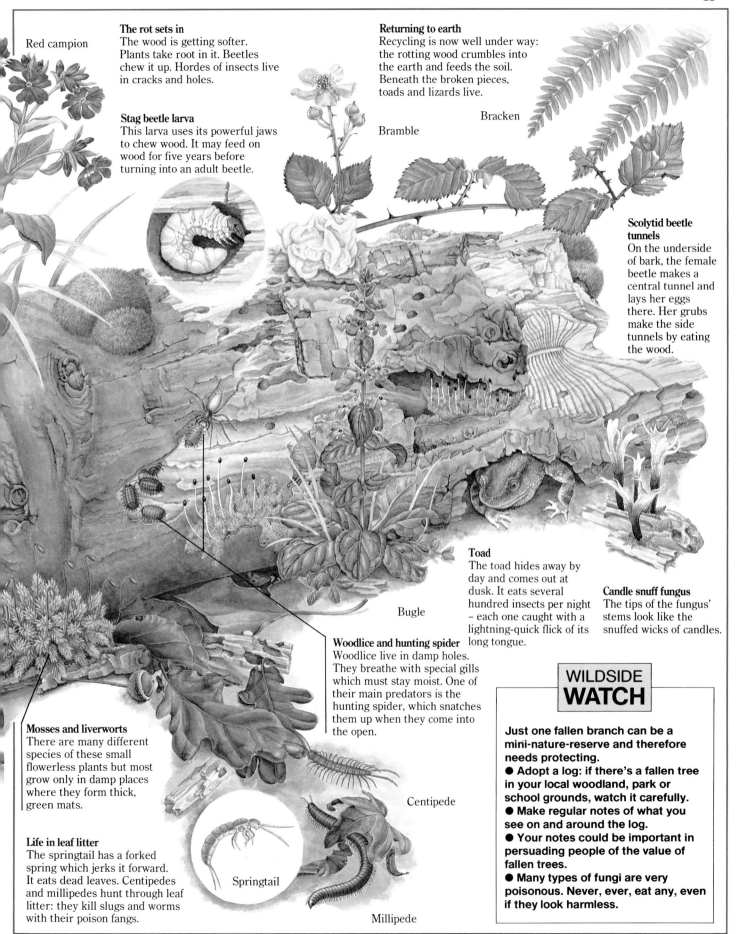

Red campion

The rot sets in
The wood is getting softer. Plants take root in it. Beetles chew it up. Hordes of insects live in cracks and holes.

Stag beetle larva
This larva uses its powerful jaws to chew wood. It may feed on wood for five years before turning into an adult beetle.

Returning to earth
Recycling is now well under way: the rotting wood crumbles into the earth and feeds the soil. Beneath the broken pieces, toads and lizards live.

Bracken

Bramble

Scolytid beetle tunnels
On the underside of bark, the female beetle makes a central tunnel and lays her eggs there. Her grubs make the side tunnels by eating the wood.

Bugle

Toad
The toad hides away by day and comes out at dusk. It eats several hundred insects per night – each one caught with a lightning-quick flick of its long tongue.

Candle snuff fungus
The tips of the fungus' stems look like the snuffed wicks of candles.

Woodlice and hunting spider
Woodlice live in damp holes. They breathe with special gills which must stay moist. One of their main predators is the hunting spider, which snatches them up when they come into the open.

Mosses and liverworts
There are many different species of these small flowerless plants but most grow only in damp places where they form thick, green mats.

Life in leaf litter
The springtail has a forked spring which jerks it forward. It eats dead leaves. Centipedes and millipedes hunt through leaf litter: they kill slugs and worms with their poison fangs.

Springtail

Centipede

Millipede

WILDSIDE WATCH

Just one fallen branch can be a mini-nature-reserve and therefore needs protecting.
● Adopt a log: if there's a fallen tree in your local woodland, park or school grounds, watch it carefully.
● Make regular notes of what you see on and around the log.
● Your notes could be important in persuading people of the value of fallen trees.
● Many types of fungi are very poisonous. Never, ever, eat any, even if they look harmless.

Fire fighters

ONE CARELESS MOMENT is all it takes. One match, one cigarette end, one spark from a campfire, can send thousands of trees up in flames. Within minutes of being set alight, a fire can get out of control. Some woodland fires blaze across many kilometres for weeks on end. Fire brigades try to put them out by flying over them in special aeroplanes which spray jets of water, and they have even tried to make it rain by shooting chemicals into the sky. But there is often nothing anyone can do.

Rising from the ashes

AFTER A BONFIRE you're left with a few half-burnt sticks and a big, black mark on the ground. Imagine that, for many kilometres. Imagine a whole lush, green woodland turned into a blackened wasteland. Tall trees are burnt to stumps, and a blanket of ash covers the ground.

It's a grim picture, but it isn't always as bad as it looks. Given a lot of time, many burnt woodlands will come back to life. Between the charred remains, fresh young shoots appear. These flowers and saplings take advantage of the open spaces left when trees burn down. And they are helped on their way by that layer of ash, which might not look very promising but actually contains nutrients to enrich the soil. Fire may kill everything in its path, but at least the next generation is ready to take over.

Through thick and thin

A TREE HAS TO STAND UP to whatever comes along. It can't seek shelter from heavy rain, cold snow or hot sun, it can't use a claw or a hand or a tail to flick away insects that eat it, and it can't run away from fire. A tree relies on its own skin to protect it.

Bark is the tree's skin. The bark of some trees is only a few millimetres thick, but others are wrapped up in 60 cm (24 in) of this cork coating. Thicker skins give more protection from fire, but even the most fire-resistant trees can still get badly burned. Some bear many scars to show the number of fires they have lived through.

Right: Fire has scorched this ponderosa pine tree, but its thick bark has saved it from getting too badly burnt.

Bursting into life

NOTHING CAN BE HEARD above the roaring flames, but when they die down the sound of something popping comes from the woodland floor. Lying there are pine cones bursting open to release the seeds inside them. The cones of some trees, such as lodgepole and jack pine, are so tightly sealed that they open only after the heat from a fire has melted them. The seeds packed inside them can stay alive for years and years before exploding into the world.

Lodgepole pine cone
A lodgepole pine cone opens and releases its seeds which fall to the ground nearby. Soon, spindly shoots grow from the seeds.

Food from the flames

ONE OF THE MOST FAMOUS wild places in the world is the Yellowstone National Park in Wyoming in the United States. Many animals such as bears, deer, chipmunks and squirrels live in its dense woodlands. But in the summer of 1988 fire swept through the park and went on burning for three months.

The leaping flames and clouds of smoke reminded many people of the story of Bambi, when a fire in the woods sends the terrified animals running for their lives. Luckily, most of the animals in Yellowstone managed to make fast getaways and escaped unhurt, although some bumped into trees because they couldn't see where they were going in the smoke.

Afterwards, the animals made the best of things. In the burnt areas birds feasted on fried insects, while bears, coyotes and badgers ate up any larger animals that had died in the fire. Beetles and birds soon found new homes in the tree stumps, and it was not too long before a fresh growth of grass and saplings provided food for deer and bison.

Above: When fire burns away the undergrowth, it exposes the hidden animals of the woodland floor - and provides rich pickings for the birds. This grey jay has found a wasps' nest, and is eating the larvae inside it.
Left: Fire may provide as well as destroy: this squirrel has discovered a welcome snack of seeds inside a burnt pine cone.

WILDSIDE WATCH

Every year, thousands of people accidentally start woodland fires that could easily be prevented.
● Whenever you visit a woodland be sure to read any notices that tell you what precautions to take to prevent fires, and what to do if fire breaks out.
● Never light a fire.
● Never even strike a match. Remember that one tiny spark is all it takes to start a big fire.
● If you see a fire starting, never try to put it out yourself. Tell an adult immediately.

Pest controllers

WE TEND TO THINK of meat-eaters, or carnivores, as large, fur-covered animals with sharp teeth. But in fact they come in all shapes and sizes, and have all sorts of ways of catching a meal.

In a woodland there are birds, small mammals, and insects all out and about after other animals. They trap them alive, snap them up, or inject them with poison. These hunters are extremely useful members of the woodland because most of their food comes in the form of insects that eat the leaves of trees. The way they keep the numbers of these 'pests' under control is more natural than the chemicals people use to kill them – and often more effective.

Well-laid traps

MANY MAGGOTS, slugs and beetles come to a sticky end by falling into traps on the woodland floor. These traps are not laid by human hands but dug by the powerful forefeet of moles. As it tunnels along underground, the mole stops every so often and digs its way to the surface, making a familiar mole-hill.

When these pop up in the middle of a golf course the moles are regarded as pests themselves – but really they should be given credit for doing their bit towards pest control.

As they snuffle through the leaf litter, shrews and hedgehogs also rank among nature's best pest controllers. Hedgehogs provide such a good service that they have been specially hired by farmers who place them in fields to gobble up crop pests.

Its enormous appetite keeps this short-tailed shrew on the go night and day, searching for insects. It is one of 200 species of shrew which hunt the floor of the world's woodlands.

Come into my parlour!

SPIDERS MIGHT NOT come top on your list of favourite animals, but in Australia they are turning out to be man's best friend. Tiny spiders are busy saving tons of apples from being eaten by caterpillars.

The caterpillars march up the apple trees and damage the fruit so badly that it has to be thrown away. Trying to kill the apple-eaters by spraying the trees with poisonous insecticide did not work, and the apple growers were at their wits' end. Finally they called in an expert. He found that trees without insecticide had loads of spiders and almost no attacked apples. Trees

The tiny combfooted spider of Australia.

with insecticide had hardly any spiders and lots of attacked apples.

It seems that the spiders catch the caterpillars by spinning webs that booby-trap them on their way up the trees. Having learnt that the chemicals were killing just the animal they needed, the apple growers stopped spraying the trees and let the spiders get on with the job of pest control.

Small but deadly

A BUG ABOUT TO tuck into the leaf of a tree suddenly finds itself attacked from all sides. Black bodies and spindly legs crawl all over it, kill it, and drag it home with them.

The attackers are wood ants, and their home is a huge dome on the woodland floor. This nest – which is half the height of a man – is made by the ants from twigs and leaves.

As many as 100,000 ants live inside one nest. They are divided into groups which each carry out different tasks. Worker ants build and repair the nest, and go out hunting. The workers of just one nest bring home thousands of insects every day. In woodlands where these ants live, the trees lose about one per cent of their leaves to insects, but in woods without the ants, the trees lose nearer 10 per cent of their leaves. So valuable are these pest controllers that in Germany and Switzerland they enjoy special protection.

Ant on guard
Some ants guard the colony from attack by insects and birds. They bite, and also curl their bodies forward and squirt formic acid.

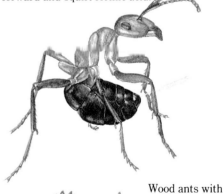

Wood ants with pine sawfly caterpillar

Big meals
Wood ants hunt for food. They work together to kill moths and caterpillars that are much larger than themselves. Then they drag their prey back to the nest.

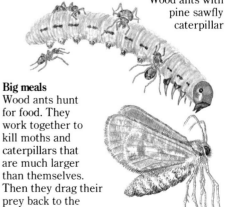

Bordered white moth

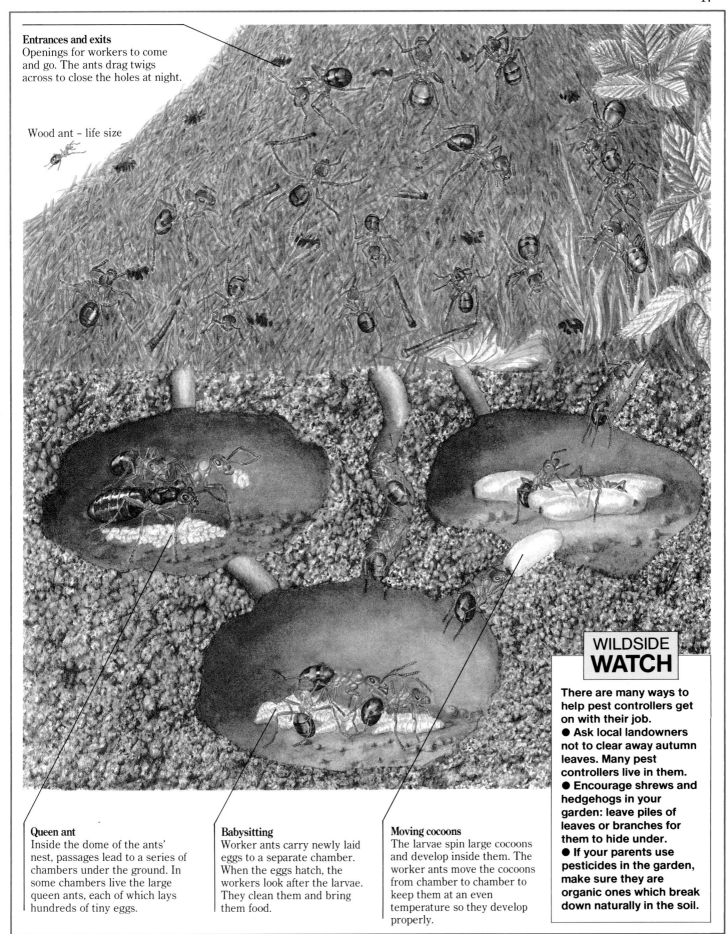

Entrances and exits
Openings for workers to come and go. The ants drag twigs across to close the holes at night.

Wood ant – life size

Queen ant
Inside the dome of the ants' nest, passages lead to a series of chambers under the ground. In some chambers live the large queen ants, each of which lays hundreds of tiny eggs.

Babysitting
Worker ants carry newly laid eggs to a separate chamber. When the eggs hatch, the workers look after the larvae. They clean them and bring them food.

Moving cocoons
The larvae spin large cocoons and develop inside them. The worker ants move the cocoons from chamber to chamber to keep them at an even temperature so they develop properly.

WILDSIDE WATCH

There are many ways to help pest controllers get on with their job.
● Ask local landowners not to clear away autumn leaves. Many pest controllers live in them.
● Encourage shrews and hedgehogs in your garden: leave piles of leaves or branches for them to hide under.
● If your parents use pesticides in the garden, make sure they are organic ones which break down naturally in the soil.

Keeping the harmony

WOODLANDS HAVE PROVIDED
people with the necessities of
life for thousands of years.
Wood has supplied fire for
warmth and light, and timber
for building. Woodland animals
and plants have provided food,
clothing and medicines. But the
woodlands can only go on
producing these supplies if
people do not damage them.

Many ancient ways of using
woodlands have proved that
people and woodlands can live
in harmony. For instance, you
don't have to kill a tree in order
to get wood from it. Trees can
be cut so that they grow again
and again, producing a con-
tinuous crop of wood.

Some human activities can
even benefit wildlife in the
woodlands. Trimming branches
creates spaces where sunlight
reaches the ground encouraging
flowers to spring up – which in
turn attract butterflies and
many other insects.

Today some of the old
methods of looking after
woodlands are coming back
into fashion because people see
they make sense.

Cutting back

HIDDEN IN THE DEPTHS of a hazelnut tree lives a small mammal with an orange coat, long tail, and black, beady eyes: the common dormouse. This shy animal sleeps in the trees all day and comes out at night. It is an expert tightrope-walker along the topmost twigs, and seldom comes to the ground.

The dormouse prefers to live in woods that people have coppiced by cutting the trees to stumps, which then sprout lots of bushy shoots. When coppicing fell out of fashion the 'common' dormouse became very rare.

Today, some trees are being coppiced again, and dormice are being given an extra helping hand by having special 'bridges' built for them. High above the ground, branches are trained to meet over open spaces, so that the tiny animals can cross over to the thickest parts of the trees.

Left: The hazel dormouse lives in tree thickets where it eats nuts and fruit. It wraps its tail around a branch and uses it, like an extra leg, to help it hold on.

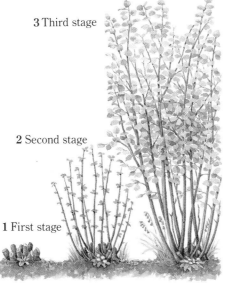

3 Third stage

2 Second stage

1 First stage

Coppicing trees
1. When a tree is coppiced, wood is taken from it without killing it. The tree is cut to a stump and left to grow again.
2. Many shoots grow from the stump, and are cut for wood. One tree can go on producing wood for hundreds of years.
3. Sometimes several trunks grow from one stump. They create thickets for birds and small mammals to live in.

High life, low life

YOU MAY BE SURPRISED to meet a sheep or cow in the middle of a wood, but they used to be a common sight because farmers often grazed their animals in woodlands. However, the cattle damaged trees and stopped the growth of branches needed for wood by eating tree shoots. But people got their own back: by regularly cutting higher branches they encouraged shoots to grow well out of the animals' reach. This system, known as pollarding, meant trees thrived, people got their wood, and animals could eat down below.

Pigs also helped themselves to food provided by woods when they were let loose to feast on acorns. These are poisonous to cattle and deer but good for pigs. This is known as 'pannage' and still occurs in some places today.

Cows can kill trees by eating the leaves and shoots. Foresters have cut these ones to make the branches grow well out of reach of the animals.

These pigs are keeping alive an old tradition. Farmers used to pay woodland owners for permission to fatten up their herds on acorns and beechmast.

WILDSIDE
WATCH

Woodland animals are being given a helping hand in many different ways.
● **Find out what is being done in woodlands and parks near you. You may be able to help on some projects.**
● **If you spot trees that look as though they used to be coppiced or pollarded, find out who owns them.**
● **Ask the owner to consider starting to trim them according to the old ways. Point out the benefits to people and animals.**

Woodland residents?

KEEP CHIPPING BITS OFF a piece of wood and in the end you will be left with nothing but a pile of splinters. So it is with a whole woodland: keep chopping down a little bit here for a housing estate, a little bit there for a factory – and just another little bit for a field of wheat – and before too long there is nothing left.

In prehistoric times, trees covered nearly two-thirds of the Earth's surface. Then, people started clearing trees to make space for settlements. Ever since, we have been taking up more and more room on the Earth at the trees' expense.

With the felling of trees goes all the wildlife that depends on them. Some plants and animals can adjust to being made homeless, but many can't. They find themselves pushed into the small pockets of natural woodland that are left. If pushed too far they become extinct.

The sad thing is, we mistakenly think that each piece of woodland we take away won't make much difference – and that there will always be natural, wild places.

Natural health

A WOODLAND UNTOUCHED by human hands looks like a tangled, ramshackle place, but really it is in perfect working order. Everything from the tallest tree to the tiniest mite plays a part in helping the woodland flourish as one living system. What makes the woodland tick is its variety. Trees of different ages, shapes and sizes all create conditions to suit many plants and animals, and each one contributes to the health of the whole.

The wild wood
This is a dense and shady world, full of hidden animals. Thick undergrowth, bushes and trees all provide food and shelter for a rich assortment of insects, birds and mammals.

Early purple orchid
The delicate early purple orchid grows only in woodlands where the conditions are just right. It needs plenty of sun, and good soil which hasn't been churned up by people and their machines.

Yellow-necked mouse
Some mice like to live in the comfort of our houses, but this one prefers sleeping rough! It's the yellow-necked mouse, and it nests in the tangled undergrowth of the wildest woods in Europe and Asia.

Disturbing the peace
Plants are pulled up and paths are cut so people can walk through woodlands. Paths loosen the soil and expose the roots of trees. Even the quietest walker disturbs animals and tramples plants.

Racoons
When people and their cars invade woodlands, some animals manage to make use of them. In North America, racoons gather by the roadside and beg for scraps of food. Normally they would be asleep in trees during the day.

Getting away from it all
Trees are felled to make way for roads which take people into the heart of the woodland. In the United States, about 300 million people visit national parks every year! Some parks now stop too many visitors coming in at once.

WILDSIDE WATCH

Wild places must be conserved: if you come across an untouched area, try not to disturb anything.
● Don't pick flowers.
● Don't drop rubbish.
● Don't let dogs chase woodland animals.
● A handy saying to remember whenever you visit a woodland: 'Take nothing but photographs, leave nothing but footprints.'

A nice place to stop

WILDERNESS AREAS are not always the havens of peace they seem. Many nature reserves are visited by millions of people every year – and once you get people, you get dogs, cars, roads, picnic places, camp sites, hotels . . . Even the most considerate visitors can't help trampling flowers, wearing away paths, and disturbing the wildlife.

Open to the public
Allowing visitors into woodlands means information centres, shops and picnic sites as well as roads. However attractive these look, they don't belong in the middle of a wilderness!

Please park here
Cars (thank goodness!) aren't usually allowed all the way into the wood. Even so, trees and other plants are bulldozed to make car parks.

Home from home
Sleeping in a tent and cooking over an open fire makes you feel closer to nature – but don't forget that you're trespassing.

Elk road sign
Woodland animals are forced on to roads to get from one part of their home to another. From tiny shrews to huge moose, thousands of them are run over every year. This sign is warning drivers in Sweden to look out for elk.

Roe deer feeding
Some of the shyest animals have turned out to be the best at living alongside people. Roe deer used to browse the trees of Europe's thickest woodlands, but with so many trees destroyed, they are forced into the open to eat grass.

City slickers

COMMON 'URBAN' animals like foxes and blue tits are the lucky ones. When their woodland homes are demolished to make way for more houses they are able to adjust their way of life and make use of gardens, the scraps found in dustbins, and any hand-outs people offer them.

Many other animals can't adapt. With each new invasion of their territory they retreat. Soon they are forced to live on small islands of woodland surrounded by a sea of civilization.

Gardening for wildlife
Gardens can be made into wildlife refuges that give back something in return for all we take from the wild.

Taking up space
Once, trees covered much of the Earth. Now only small pieces of woodland are left, surrounded by towns and cities.

Fox
Most woodland hunters, like the wolf and the lynx, have retreated into the last pieces of wilderness – but throughout Europe and North America the red fox has changed its way of life to fit in with human beings. It raids dustbins, and has even been known to help itself to catfood!

Blue tit
Some woodland birds depend on people putting food out for them, but in Britain, the blue tit doesn't wait for these hand-outs. It pecks open the lids of milk bottles delivered to doorsteps each morning.

Living off the land
Fields, as well as houses and factories, replace trees. Some birds can't live outside woodlands, but sparrows and wood pigeons raid the crops.

WILDSIDE WATCH

Whether you live in an old house or a new flat, you may still be able to find signs of its original site.
● Find out what was there before your home was built: contact your local planning department or library.
● For the future, keep an eye out for new developments that threaten trees: some organisations campaign to save trees from the chop.

Harvesting trees

IN THE SIXTEENTH CENTURY someone hit on the idea of *growing* trees for their wood. Tree seeds could be sown, left to grow, and harvested. So 'tree farming' began – but it didn't really take off until this century.

Nowadays, more and more people want more and more wood and paper, so more and more trees are planted. The way it is done can spell trouble for the natural world.

Before trees are planted, land must be cleared for them, so whole moorlands and natural woodlands are destroyed. Rows of exactly the same kind of tree are put in their place and there isn't much chance for anything else to live there. Plantations like these cloak mile after mile of northern Europe and North America.

Some foresters are starting to grow a more natural mixture of trees. In the long run this gives them better wood – and creates better places for plants and animals.

Coniferous forestry

MOST TREES PLANTED FOR timber are conifers. They can grow just about anywhere, they grow fast, and their long, straight trunks are easy to saw into planks. Also, their wood is good for pulping to make paper.

Seedlings are planted close together in straight rows. Any young trees that die or any that grow faster than the rest are replaced.

This keeps everything tidy and easy to manage. When the trees get a bit bigger their low, side branches are lopped off so the wood will look smooth and knot-free.

The trees, all the same size and shape, are cut down at the same time. Then the ground is treated with chemical fertiliser and a new batch of conifer seedlings is planted.

Other plantations

TREES ARE NOT ONLY GROWN for their wood. They also provide us with products, from fruits and nuts to oils and rubber. Most of these trees do not need to be cut down to get what we want from them. Earlier methods of cutting into trunks to extract substances did kill trees, but modern techniques let them live. Latex to make rubber, and resin to make turpentine come from living trees by making incisions into them.

Some trees are even skinned alive! Bark from the cork oak tree is regularly removed with no ill effects to the tree. Bottle stoppers, shoe soles and insulation materials all come from cork oaks.

Cork oak trees have been cultivated in the eastern Mediterranean for 2000 years. Their bark is removed to be made into cork products; the trees soon grow a new layer.

Conifer trees grown for timber are planted in narrow, straight rows. The aim is to produce the most timber in the shortest possible time. Each batch is ready to be cut down every 30–50 years.

Young trees

RANKS OF TALL TREES offer little in the way of food and shelter for animals, and make it too dark for ground plants to grow. Young plantations allow wildlife more of a chance, but are not as rich as a natural woodland.

Some animals do well in plantations but are often not welcomed by foresters – in the same way that farmers dislike plants that compete with their produce or animals that eat it. But foresters do encourage some of the larger animals, such as wild cats and pine martens, because they eat small mammals like voles and rabbits that destroy young trees.

Above: The wildcat once lived throughout the woodlands of Britain, but was so persecuted that it nearly became extinct. Now it is found only in Scotland, where it is popular with foresters because it catches rabbits and voles which eat tree seedlings.
Left: When they climb conifers and gnaw the bark, porcupines can kill trees. They are a serious nuisance in some North American plantations.
Right: The crested tit prefers natural coniferous woodland to plantations: it needs a good supply of old, rotting trees to nest in.

WILDSIDE
WATCH

Everyone can help to save trees by re-using paper as often as possible. Think of all the paper items, cups and envelopes, for example, that most of us use just once and then throw away.
● Re-use envelopes and paper.
● Save newspapers for recycling and encourage your friends to do the same.
● Find out the uses to which different types of trees are put.

Deer destroyers

DEER FIT INTO WOODLANDS perfectly. Some are to be found grazing in clearings, others stick to thickets where they browse leaves and twigs. Many are hardly ever seen at all, for deer are some of the shyest animals. Even so, most of the 40 species across the world have had a lot of contact with people.

Although their speed and beauty has been much admired, deer have also been hunted since the earliest times. At first they provided people with meat and skins, and their antlers were used as tools. Nowadays many are hunted just for sport, and some are killed because their eating habits endanger plants and trees. We have had the power of life or death over deer for centuries – and still have that power today.

Destructive habits

LITTLE IS LEFT ALIVE in parts of some woodlands when deer have had their fill. Half-eaten leaves, shoots and buds lie scattered on the ground, young trees are nibbled to nothing, and older ones are stripped of everything within reach, including their bark. The only way to save the woodlands is to kill the deer. Thousands are shot every year – but it's not really their fault that they wreak such havoc.

Deer can eat their way through a great deal of plant life. Normally, however, there are not enough of them to do any serious harm. The trouble starts when there are too many mouths to feed – and *that* is caused by people upsetting the natural balance of the woodland. To begin with, we've killed off many of the animals which eat deer. In Scotland, for instance, where there are more red deer than ever before, the last wolf was killed in 1740. On top of that, we have taken over so much of the deers' land that they have to go looking for food. They eat up the last bits of natural woodland and stray into timber plantations and farms. Some have even developed a taste for garden roses.

A young roe deer makes a meal of some leaves. Deer are peaceful browsers – but they can wreck woodlands by eating all the trees to death.

The bark of this birch tree has been bitten off and eaten by fallow deer. They cause the death of many trees in this way.

On the brink of extinction

MANY A HUNTER has stories to tell of the times he has tried to sneak up on a deer, only to watch it bound away. In the woodlands of North America, this often means seeing nothing but a white flash as a white-tailed deer disappears. American Indians used to hunt these deer for meat, and for skins to make clothing. Later, the white settlers wanted these products too, so many more deer were killed. In some places they became so scarce that hunting was stopped, but numbers have risen again, and they are now shot for sport.

Some other species of deer have not been given a similar second chance. Hunting and the destruction of their homes has put 12 of them in danger of extinction.

Below: The most endangered deer in the world. Hunting and habitat destruction have reduced the number of Manipur brow-antlered deer to less than 20 animals. They live in a national park in India.

A costly scent

THE MOST EXPENSIVE animal product in the world is not a rare fur, or even something special to eat. It is a strong-smelling sort of jelly which dries to form a black powder. Called musk, it is used to make perfumes and medicines, and is more valuable than gold. It comes from the musk deer which lives in the woodlands of central and north-eastern Asia. So many of these animals have been killed for their musk that they are now in danger of dying out altogether. Only the adult males produce the musk, but many females and young die when they are caught in traps set for the males.

Musk deer have no antlers to clash, but the males fight with their tusks. Now, the guns and traps of human hunters have wiped most of them out.

WILDSIDE WATCH

Deer are hunted to provide us with all sorts of things from leather to cures for asthma.

● Think up a list of everyday objects which come from deer and other animals.

● Develop your list into a quiz: ask people to match the product with the animal.

● Find out more about animals which, like deer, are killed because they harm other living things. Badgers and foxes are put to death for spreading disease, and rabbits for eating too much vegetation.

Woodland invaders

MOST WOODLANDS OF THE WORLD are in danger of being occupied by foreign plants and animals. There are already European boars and English sparrows in America, and American deer are over-running New Zealand. Many invaders take over an area and push out the residents.

Most invaders are helped by people who release animals sometimes on purpose and sometimes accidentally – when, for example, they escape from cages or farms. There are also stowaways – rats, mice and insects – on ships and planes.

When foreign plants are grown in parks and gardens they often don't stay put for long. Their seeds hitch rides on the wind, or on the fur of animals, or even on the soles of people's shoes. Plants are some of the most successful invaders.

Grey areas

THERE'S A LOT MORE to squirrels than bright eyes and bushy tails. In fact, these tree-dwelling, nut-cracking creatures are the subjects of a thorough scientific investigation that involves both murder and mystery.

The story begins 100 years ago, when grey squirrels from North America were first let loose in Britain. As soon as they set foot on British soil they began to over-run the country. Now there is hardly a woodland anywhere that these invaders have not occupied.

The greys look quite harmless, but they kill trees by eating bark and shoots.

They have moreover been accused of murdering red squirrels, which began disappearing from British woods when the greys came along. However, no one could prove the greys were guilty, and in some places they were found living peacefully with the reds.

Next, the greys were blamed for infecting the reds with a deadly disease, but again there was no proof. Much of the mystery of the disappearing reds remains unsolved, but the current line of enquiry is leading to the nuts that both squirrels eat. It seems that the greys are probably stealing food from under the reds' noses.

Right: Many woodland mammals only come out at night, but squirrels are up and about in broad daylight. The North American grey squirrel is often seen in British woodlands – and in gardens where it raids peanuts put out for the birds.
Inset: The red squirrel spends a lot of time collecting nuts – although snails, insects and birds' eggs also feature on its menu. It lives in the woodlands of Europe and northern Asia, but has become extremely rare in Britain.

Immigrants

THE BLACK CLOUDS that suddenly fill the sky do not mean rain, but birds. Millions of them. They are European starlings on their way to roost in a North American woodland.

There was not one starling in sight in the United States until 40 pairs were released by a man who believed that all the birds mentioned in the works of Shakespeare should have the right to fly in American air. Just 90 years later they are one of the commonest birds.

When great numbers of starlings perch together, branches break under the sheer weight, and trees are poisoned by their droppings. They also take over the nest holes of bluebirds and woodpeckers, leaving these rightful owners with nowhere to go.

Birds of a feather flock together! In the case of European starlings, that can mean over a million birds in one flock. They fill the skies of North America as well as Europe.

The bountiful black locust tree

WHEN BEES ARE OUT and about in search of nectar, the black locust tree offers them plenty of flowers to dip into. This bountiful provider is now common in Europe, but comes from North America.

The black locust was first planted in Europe because it is good to look at. It then made itself useful by feeding the bees and providing people with wood. Its seeds soon spread, and the trees advanced across large areas.

This is good news for bees, but bad news for other animals because the trees upset the natural balance of established woodlands and make it difficult for resident wildlife to go on living there.

Other introduced trees and small plants have caused similar trouble all over the world. Even the normally harmless michaelmas daisy has been known to do battle with resident plants in some places.

The flowers of the black locust tree provide the honey bee with plenty of nectar to drink.

WILDSIDE WATCH

Track down the invaders in your local woodland!
● **Visit a wood and make a list of familiar plants and animals.**
● **Find out which ones are native and which have been introduced.**
● **Help native plants by growing wildflowers in a corner of your garden or school grounds.**
● **Grow trees as well as wildflowers. Plant only species which grow naturally in your area.**

Landscape gardeners

ALL WOODLANDS CONTAIN countless pairs of teeth hard at work eating the trees. Tiny insects nibble away at the edges of leaves, while larger vegetarians, such as deer and antelope, munch their way through whole bunches. Other animals peel and eat bark, or chew through wood, and many feast on nuts and flowers.

Being slowly eaten alive doesn't do a tree much good, but most trees are built to withstand a certain amount of attack. One oak tree, for example, can be eaten by hundreds of different kinds of insect, and still live to a ripe old age of several centuries.

But sometimes animals do kill trees and change the whole landscape from woodland to open grassland or even desert. This usually happens when there are too many mouths to feed in one small area of woodland. And *that* usually happens when people cut down so many trees that the animals have only a few to live on.

A huge appetite

ELEPHANTS ARE VERY GOOD at eating all their greens. In fact, one 4-tonne elephant gets through 227 kg (60 lb) of vegetation every single day.

In Africa, elephants like to eat grass, but in the dry season the grass withers and the elephants turn their attention to trees. They eat twigs and branches, bark, flowers, fruits and leaves. They head-butt trees in order to knock them down, rip into them with their tusks, and pull them up using their trunks.

Elephants used to kill some trees and then move on, giving the woodland a chance to recover. Nowadays, people have destroyed many places where elephants live. They are therefore forced to stay in the small areas that are left, and to eat everything they can find. This means they kill all the trees, and change whole woodlands into nothing but bare plains.

When they are especially hungry, African elephants eat their way through trees. In the process, they kill whole stretches of woodland.

Killer Disease

LITTLE BEETLES have managed to change the look of large areas of Europe and North America by wiping out the trees. Twenty-three million elm trees used to tower over southern Britain, but now you would be hard pressed to find any at all. It's a similar story in other places such as France, where all the 20,000 elms that used to be found in Paris have disappeared.

The beetles live and feed on the elms but are not actually the killers. As they go from tree to tree they carry a deadly fungus that attacks the tree very quickly. The tree tries to fight back by producing a gummy substance, but this only blocks up its insides and it dies within months.

No one knows where the fungus came from, but the disease was first identified in Holland, which is why it is known as Dutch Elm Disease. Efforts to stop it spreading by getting rid of the beetles have not worked. One tree may be home to thousands of beetles, all carrying the killer.

How Dutch Elm Disease spreads
Bark beetles spread the disease by carrying it from tree to tree. When the female lays her eggs on a diseased elm, she picks up the disease and passes it to all the other elms that she visits. When her eggs hatch, the larvae make tunnels under the bark and eat the wood. As adults they fly to other elms and take the disease with them.

Eating up the trees!

WHETHER OR NOT goats live up to their reputation for eating anything and everything, one thing's for sure: they do eat trees. Mostly they munch through leaves, but fresh shoots, whole saplings, and long strips of bark all go down well.

Goats can live almost anywhere, and they provide lots of meat, milk and wool – all of which makes them popular domestic animals.

But their eating habits make them unpopular. In some places goats have killed so many trees that they have turned lush woodlands into dry, dusty deserts. These destroyers are usually goats that have become wild and built up their numbers until there are too many living in one area. Then they eat everything within reach – which includes the top branches, as goats can climb trees.

Goat supporters say that the animals only add the 'finishing touches' to work done by people in clearing away trees.

WILDSIDE WATCH

Human beings are the most devastating landscape gardeners in the world. Just one person can use up the equivalent of at least two trees a year. You can help leave trees where they are by using less paper.
- **Cut down on the amount you use.**
- **Avoid buying anything which is over-packaged.**
- **Always use both sides of a sheet of paper.**
- **Don't automatically accept a bag with everything you buy.**

A goat enjoys the high life! Goats have hooves which can grasp branches – so they climb trees in search of food.

34

Poison from the skies

LOOKING PALE, FEELING TIRED, and losing weight are all ways our bodies let us know that something is wrong. Trees also fall ill. They droop, their branches grow in peculiar shapes, and their leaves turn yellow.

Sometimes it is difficult to find out what is causing an illness, but one thing is clear: whole woodlands are being slowly poisoned to death by people. We're not doing it on purpose, but it's caused by all the pollution we send into the air.

Whenever factories burn fossil fuels such as oil and coal, poisonous gases are released into the air. Cars and lorries also give off poisonous fumes. These gases dissolve in rain and fall as harmful acids. Normal rain contains about as much acid as orange juice, but acid rain is stronger than vinegar. This invisible killer is attacking fish in lakes and rivers, making ancient stone buildings crumble, and devastating large areas of woodland.

The Black Forest

A THICK GREEN CLOAK of trees lies over part of Germany. It is known as the Black Forest, and it used to be home to a whole range of animals, including pine martens and wildcats, owls and woodpeckers. But now the animals have disappeared from large parts of this forest, and in some places the trees are nothing but giant sticks poking up from the ground. Their deaths are caused by acid rain and other pollution in the air.

The Black Forest is one of the hardest hit areas, but large stretches of woodland in central Europe, Sweden and Norway, and eastern North America are also dying. Some types of tree are more likely to be affected than others – and they don't have to be near any factories or cities to suffer. The pollution gets carried by the wind from country to country. Britain is responsible for much of the acid rain that falls in Norway, and maple trees in Canada receive large doses from the United States.

Above: Acid rain is killing these trees in Poland. The same thing is happening to whole forests in other parts of Europe and North America. This pollution is one of the most serious threats to woodlands today.
Left: Lichen likes healthy trees – so plenty of it is a good sign. It grows on bark and does no harm, but can't survive in heavily polluted areas.

Acid attack

ACID RAIN ATTACKS a tree in two ways. First, it eats away at the leaves by stripping off their waxy surface. Without this protective coating the leaves easily catch diseases or just dry up and die.

The second way that acid rain kills trees is by poisoning their food and water supplies. The roots of a tree not only anchor it in the earth, but also suck up water, minerals and nutrients from the soil. These are drawn up into the tree and circulated inside it. When acid rain soaks into the soil it dissolves many of the essential nutrients – such as calcium and magnesium – and washes them away. It also changes the make-up of the soil by encouraging dangerous toxins to build up in it. The tree slowly dies from starvation and poisoning.

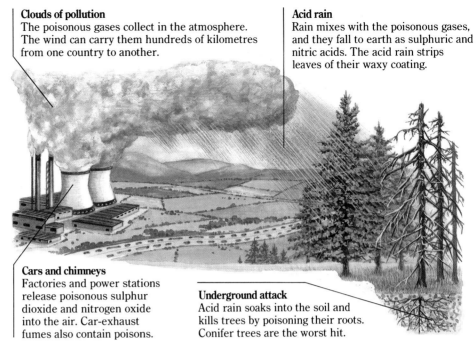

Clouds of pollution
The poisonous gases collect in the atmosphere. The wind can carry them hundreds of kilometres from one country to another.

Acid rain
Rain mixes with the poisonous gases, and they fall to earth as sulphuric and nitric acids. The acid rain strips leaves of their waxy coating.

Cars and chimneys
Factories and power stations release poisonous sulphur dioxide and nitrogen oxide into the air. Car-exhaust fumes also contain poisons.

Underground attack
Acid rain soaks into the soil and kills trees by poisoning their roots. Conifer trees are the worst hit.

Red alert!

GUIDE DOGS AND POLICE DOGS are well known for spending their lives helping people, but now earthworms and honey bees are doing their bit – by joining the fight against pollution! One problem with acid rain and other pollutants is that you can't see them coming. By the time trees show signs of illness, it is often too late to do anything about it.

Recently, scientists have turned to animals to find out what's going on.

Some animals pick up poisons very quickly, so by giving them regular check-ups, the scientists can take action as soon as they find anything wrong. If the pollution can be stopped in time, a whole woodland may be saved.

Earthworms are excellent early warning systems because they live in the soil *and* eat it, so they soon fall ill if it is contaminated. Honey bees catch tiny particles of pollution on their hairy bodies, and swallow it when they drink nectar from flowers.

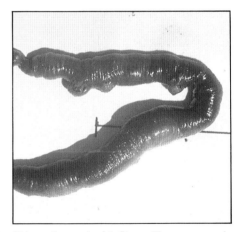

This earthworm is sick. Its swellings are caused by pollution in the soil.

Honey bees don't only live in man-made hives! Trees are their natural home, and they are important pollinators of woodland plants. Their usefulness to people goes further than the production of honey; they also help monitor pollution.

WILDSIDE WATCH

Acid rain could become 10 times worse by the year 2000 unless urgent action is taken. The worst offenders are power stations, which need to control the amount of poison they pump out, but we can all cut down on pollution by conserving energy.
● We should not leave lights on unnecessarily.
● We should not waste hot water.
● We should insulate our buildings and not overheat them.
● We should use unleaded petrol and have catalytic converters installed in our cars.

Going underground

SOME ANIMALS manage to keep well out of sight even when they are living right under our noses. Badgers don't show their famous black-and-white faces very often; yet they are found in woodlands nearly all over the world. Basically, badgers like to keep themselves to themselves. They spend their days below ground, and emerge under cover of darkness. But even such secretive animals have not escaped our attention. People have burdened them with problems, including trapping them for fur, building on top of their homes, and poisoning them when they dig up gardens.

Badgering badgers

GLOBE-TROTTING is definitely not in a badger's scheme of things. A badger spends its life at home with the family. All we see of a badger's set is a hole in the ground, but that hole leads to a maze of corridors and chambers. They are occupied by generation after generation, and the current owners are always digging away to improve and enlarge the accommodation.

Badgers are not the only ones busy extending their living quarters. People are taking more and more land for themselves. When woods are turned into building sites, the badgers' homes are bulldozed. Often the animals try to repair the damage, and stay on, but living near people is full of hazards. It's hard to find food and shelter amongst roads and buildings. Even badgers still living in woodlands are not left alone. They are poisoned and shot merely to get rid of them. And they are dug out of their homes and forced to fight with dogs as a sport for people to watch.

Home and territory
Badgers seek secluded spots in copses, hedgerows and woods. They dig a maze of tunnels and burrows to live in. Above ground, they always follow the same paths through their territory.

Family life
Several families live together. Each female looks after her own cubs. At first she keeps them in a chamber underground. They come into the open when they are about six weeks old.

Finding food
At twilight, badgers come out to feed in fields and clearings. They eat beetles, nuts, berries and voles – but mainly earthworms. One badger can eat 200 worms in one night.

Urban badgers
Roads cut into woodlands. Houses are built where the badgers live. The badgers may stay put, but they face many hazards. They fall into swimming-pools and are poisoned for digging up gardens. But some people put food out for them.

Housing developments threaten badgers' habitats.

Cars' headlights are picked up by roadside reflectors which warn badgers of oncoming traffic.

Badger tunnel

Reflector

Fresh from the farm
Farms take over the badgers' territory. The badgers help farmers by eating rabbits and insects which damage crops – but badgers also raid fields of corn, oats and strawberries.

Accident prevention
Many badgers get run over. Ways of preventing this include subways to divert the animals under the road, and reflectors which warn them when cars are coming. The reflectors pick up light from car headlights and shine it on to the sides of the road where the badgers are about to cross.

Badger paths

WALKING IN THE WOODS, you may come across narrow trails winding through the undergrowth. These belong to badgers. Like us, they get to know the best ways round their neighbourhood, and use them all the time. Many roads cut across the badger paths, and very many animals get run over. The least we can do is to help them to the other side. Traffic lights and pedestrian crossings wouldn't be much use, but we *can* provide them with their own 'subways'.

One or other of the nine species of badger is found everywhere except in Antarctica and Australasia. This one is the American badger. It is such a strong digger that it can break into the hard surface of a road.

WILDSIDE WATCH

There are lots of ways that you can help your local badgers.
● Read up on badger behaviour and then look for signs of their presence.
● Some local badger protection groups organise people to watch particular sets and make sure they're not disturbed. Find out if you can help.
● If roads are being planned near badgers, write to conservation organisations for information about special badger tunnels and present it to the planners.

Bear necessities

BASICALLY, THE BEAR NECESSITY of life is food. Lots of it. Bears spend most of their time eating, sleeping off their last meal, or looking for the next one. It's not that they're greedy, but they *are* big, and they *do* have rather large appetites. Most of their diet consists of nuts, berries, fruit and grass, and a bear has to eat piles of this vegetarian food in order to keep going.

The need for food is related to the need for space. Each bear needs to roam across a large area to find enough to feed itself. Just one grizzly bear, for example, likes to have a massive 30 sq. km (11½ square miles) to itself.

In the past, when so much of the Earth was covered in woodlands, there was plenty of room for bears. Nowadays, most woodlands have been cut down. With them have gone the bears. They have completely died out in many places, and are now found only in specially protected woodlands. Even here their future is not always secure.

Barely protected

ONE WAY TO SAVE BEARS from dying out is to leave them alone in the wild. Most bears like to live in very dense woodland where there is plenty of food and shelter. Some, like the Indian sloth bear and the Asian black bear, are now very rare because most of their habitat has been cut down.

It's the same story for brown bears. Three thousand years ago these big, shaggy animals wandered right through Great Britain and the rest of Europe. By 1990, there were only a few hundred left in France, Spain and Italy. Only in the wildest parts of Russia and Scandinavia do large numbers of brown bears still live.

Most brown bears live in protected areas, but these are not always big enough for them. When the bears can't find enough food they raid nearby farms. One bear can wreck a field of wheat or sugar beet in no time. In Italy, farmers are paid compensation for damage, and, in one reserve, food is specially grown for the bears.

Top right: Helped by strong claws which give them a good grip, bears are expert climbers. In the trees, they find plenty of food such as nuts, fruit and insects. This Asian black bear cub is helping itself to a tasty twig.
Right: Without a care in the world, European brown bears indulge in a game. But their dwindling numbers are causing serious concern.

Grizzly problems

EVERY YEAR millions of people in North America escape the hurly-burly of towns and cities by visiting nature reserves. Some of these are in woodlands where the last remaining grizzly bears live. When the reserves were first set up, food was put out for the bears to make them come into the open so visitors could see them. The bears soon became a big tourist attraction. But they soon became a big problem too.

The trouble was that the bears couldn't tell the difference between food for them and food for people.

Bears have a very good sense of smell, and easily picked up the smell of meals being cooked by people camping in the parks – so they just followed their noses right into camp sites and helped themselves. Now they have the habit, and also regularly raid rubbish bins for leftover picnics.

Not many bears actually harm people, but these huge, half-tonne wild animals can do a lot of damage and are not always welcome. So now people are trying to solve a problem they have brought upon themselves: having lured the bears to them, they now have to make them go away. Some bears are simply killed, but others are captured and removed from the camp sites. The latest tricks to persuade the bears to leave include scaring them with loud noises and squirting them in the face with peppery sauce. Some bears are even being sent on a training course to teach them to run in the opposite direction whenever they catch sight of a person – especially a person eating dinner.

Below left: The grizzly bear is one of the largest and strongest land animals, and needs fear no predators - except human beings. This trespasser may be punished with death, but the grizzlies were living here long before the holiday homes were built.
Below: Being 'smarter than the average bear', Yogi bear always provides his own picnic. Real bears steal food from people.

WILDSIDE WATCH

Bears like our leftovers but many different animals run into problems when they come across our litter.
● **After a picnic, be sure to take all your rubbish and leftovers home.**
● **Always cut up plastic rings from packs of drinks. They throttle birds and mammals if they get stuck round their necks.**
● **Wrap sharp things in newspaper – their edges can cut.**
● **Take all glass bottles to a bottle bank. This saves mice and shrews from getting stuck inside them, *and* helps conserve the Earth's resources.**

Helping hawks

WITH ITS SHARP EYESIGHT, curved claws and hooked beak, the sparrowhawk is perfectly built for hunting down the small birds it eats. As the bird shoots out of the sky and catches something in its talons, it seems as if nothing and no one could get in its way. But thanks to the actions of people, these beautiful birds of prey – and others like them – are hovering on the brink of extinction.

How they come to be in such peril is an example of just how much harm can be done when people tamper with nature. In this case, the birds of prey are endangered because people put poisonous chemicals on fields.

Storing up poisons

HUGE NUMBERS of large, woodland-dwelling, meat-eating birds are being killed by chemicals put on fields of crops to get rid of tiny insects.

After killing the pests, the poisons stay around. They get into the crops, whose seeds are eaten by birds such as sparrows and thrushes. Swallowing poisoned food doesn't usually kill a seed-eater; instead, the poisons get stored in its body – so the more poisoned food it eats, the more poison builds up inside it.

Seed-eating birds are the favourite food of bigger birds such as goshawks and sparrowhawks. With each mouthful of meat, these birds of prey also take in large doses of poison, which builds up inside them until they die.

Right: Its markings make the sparrowhawk hard to see when it swoops through the trees and hunts small birds. Eating birds contaminated by farm chemicals killed many sparrowhawks – but some countries have banned these poisons, and the sparrowhawks are returning.

Preying on success

JUST IN THE nick of time one bird of prey that was once widespread has been saved from extinction. When farmers started using especially harmful chemicals, so many peregrine falcons were poisoned as a result that they nearly all died out.

Luckily, a scientist in Canada saw how serious things were, and started breeding the birds in captivity. This had never been done before, but he learnt how to look after the chicks by watching wild birds.

Now, every spring, young birds are put back into the wild – but first the places where they are released are checked to make sure no pesticides are used anywhere nearby.

Above: A baby peregrine falcon being fed. The chick was born in captivity as part of a project to save this species from extinction. It will be released into the wild when it is old enough to look after itself.
Left: This unborn chick has been crushed to death because its shell is too thin. The pesticides inside its mother's body made her unable to form a proper shell.

WILDSIDE WATCH

● Find out about organic farming. How are pests got rid of without the use of pesticides? Would there be enough food to go round if everyone farmed organically?
● Buy organic food.

● Don't use poisons in your garden: there are safe alternatives.
● Find out about agrisilviculture, a method of growing food between trees that prevents the soil blowing away.

Night fliers

AT NIGHT NO WOODLAND would be complete without owls. Most birds go to sleep when darkness falls, but at night the owl gets up for breakfast.

With its plump body and big, round eyes, this night hunter is a well-known animal; but did you know that there are more than 130 different kinds of owl? There are owls as small as sparrows and as big as eagles. There are owls that come out in daylight, owls that live in the desert, and owls that live underground. *And* there are probably owls alive that no one knows about at all. A new species is discovered about every 10 years!

But owls are also dying out. The reason is simple: most owls live in woodlands. When woodlands are cleared away, the owls go too.

Dangerous flight paths

MODERN CIVILIZATION doesn't make life any easier for owls. In fact, it can be disastrous for them. Many low-flying owls get hit by cars, some die when they fly into electricity power lines, and some owls are deliberately shot. With people and their machines almost everywhere, owls can't escape the modern world. Some find it easier than others to cope.

The biggest problem facing owls is that people keep taking away their homes. When woodlands are destroyed, owls are left high and dry. Some – like the tawny owl – take up residence wherever they can find trees in parks and gardens, and even nest on the ground. Tawny owls have also managed to change their menu. In woodlands they eat mice and voles, but in towns they mostly feed on house sparrows.

The magnificent eagle owl – the largest owl in Europe – is not so lucky. It was once quite common but now only lives in woods that people, their cars and their guns can't get to.

Above: Life in the fast lane suits the tawny owl, but there is a price to pay. Many get run over when they hunt mice and voles which live amongst the wild plants on roadside verges.
Left: The European eagle owl has died out from many woodlands – it has been heavily hunted, and its eggs have been stolen by egg collectors. Now strictly protected, its numbers are slowly increasing.

The northern spotted owl

ONE OWL WHICH LIKES to keep itself to itself is the northern spotted owl. It lives in the thickest part of the woods in a corner of North America, and is hardly ever seen. Yet just recently this shy bird has become the centre of attention. It is the subject of heated arguments between people who disagree over its future: one group wants to destroy the woods where the owl lives, and the other group wants to save the woods, the owl, and all the other animals and plants living there. These woods are especially important because they contain some of the oldest trees left in North America. Many are over 250 years old. The northern spotted owl lives in these ancient trees and nowhere else. If the remaining trees are cut down, the owl will become extinct. At the moment, plans are being put forward to cut down some trees but leave others for the owls. With luck, the humans will come to some agreement before it's too late for this particular owl.

Above: Excellent eyesight and hearing make the owl a master hunter. This northern spotted owl takes off in search of flying squirrels and red tree voles. The destruction of its woodland home in the Pacific Northwest of North America has left this owl hovering on the brink of extinction.

WILDSIDE WATCH

Here's how you can help owls.
● We mostly think of bird boxes as being for small birds, but there are owl boxes too. Find out which owls live in your neighbourhood and put up an appropriate box in a quiet part of the garden or nearby park.
● If you come across baby owls on their own, leave them alone. They are probably not orphans, but have been left while their parents find food.
● Find out if there are any local conservation projects that you can join which protect owls.

Vicious villains

EVERY YEAR, hordes of bloodthirsty killers claim one million human victims, and no one knows how many animals. All they do is drink a little blood and then buzz off. But mosquitoes and other insects pass on many diseases when they bite, and are far more dangerous than all the big meat-eaters put together.

Yet animals such as lynxes and cougars get the blame for being fierce murderers. Out of dislike for them, people shoot them, poison them, and trap them. Now we're beginning to see that these animals are important members of the woodland; but we still have some way to go before welcoming them with open arms.

Cats of the wild

APART FROM ITS EAR TUFTS and sideburns, the lynx looks like an overgrown tabby cat – and in some ways that's what it is. Both are stealthy, night-time hunters. The difference is that pet cats are fed meat from a tin, and wild ones have to go and catch their meal. Woodland cats such as the lynx, bobcat and cougar, have to work hard. Everything from a mouse to a deer is wary of them, and many a time they watch their dinner getting away. They usually only manage to catch old, young, or sick animals, and often go hungry.

It's a good job they do catch some prey, because wild cats help to keep down the number of animals that eat trees and other plants. Too many of these vegetarians can kill a woodland by eating it to death. Far from being a menace, the big meat-eaters can actually save the life of a woodland.

The lynx rests by day and hunts by night. This one looks as if butter wouldn't melt in its mouth, but lynx have a bad reputation because they steal sheep.

Foxing the foxes

IN PARTS OF EUROPE, helicopters drop bombs on woodland. Their targets are foxes, but don't worry: the bombs contain medicine, not explosives. Foxes carry a nasty disease called rabies, which can be passed on to dogs and people. Whenever there is a rabies outbreak, thousands of foxes are killed. Now the plan is to stop them getting the disease by vaccinating them. The bombs are the equivalent of an injection in your arm. The foxes snap up their medicine as it tastes like fish, which they find irresistible.

Getting rid of rabies will help to make the fox more popular, but he's been in our bad books for a long time. Sly, fictional foxes are found in fables and folk stories. Real ones that raid hen houses are accused of being thieves and murderers – so it may be a while before the fox clears his name.

Caught red-handed

IT'S NOT OFTEN that a criminal gets caught red-handed, but in early 1990 a man was seen breaking the law by setting a trap to kill birds such as owls and sparrowhawks. They are tracked down because they eat animals that people want to shoot for sport. In many countries it is now illegal to kill the birds. People were once *rewarded* for doing so. Even kingfishers had a price on their heads because they were depriving fishermen of their catch!

A thief makes a quick getaway. But is it fair to shoot the fox for committing this crime?

A tawny owl dies slowly in a pole trap. This cruel method of killing has been illegal for many years, but is still used today.

What's in a name?

SUPER WEASEL, devil bear, and glutton are the nicknames of an animal often described as one of the most ferocious beasts alive. It's the wolverine, and it lives in the remotest woodlands of Europe and North America. But it doesn't live up to its reputation at all. Wolverines *are* strong, and *can* stand up to animals bigger than themselves, but they don't go looking for trouble. Now that their true life story is coming out, perhaps people will stop hounding them.

Having a fine set of teeth doesn't make the wolverine a fierce killer. In fact, this ferocious-looking animal leads quite a hard life - wandering the coldest woodlands in search of something to eat.

WILDSIDE WATCH

● Suggest your class puts together a project to show how some animals have been misunderstood.
● As part of the project, collect pictures from magazines, newspapers and comics, showing the animals as fierce and nasty. Point out that these are the images that most people see.
● Remind anyone who keeps chickens or pet rabbits to make sure their cages are fox-proof.

The big bad...

EVERYONE LOVES TO HATE the big, bad wolf. Almost everywhere he goes he's Public Enemy Number One. In popular imagination, this powerful beast lopes through the wildest places on Earth gnashing his teeth. He's out to murder every innocent creature he comes across – including a nice, juicy person. What's more, he gangs up with other wolves and they all howl blood-curdling war-cries before going on the rampage.

A different picture is painted by people who know about wolves. They explain that wolves don't eat human flesh, and live peacefully together, abiding by strict rules of behaviour. Youngsters are playful, but polite to their elders. Grown-ups are responsible leaders and good parents. They *do* eat other animals, but so do many other animals, and so do many people . . .

Wolves of the future

WOLVES ARE VERY definitely at the mercy of people, not the other way round. Their future lies in our hands.

In some places, things are looking up for wolves. Restrictions on hunting them in parts of North America, Spain and Portugal have led to an increase in their numbers. This is the first step, but it won't do them much good unless wild areas are set aside for them. If this doesn't happen, the wolves will live too close for comfort to people and their livestock, and the whole problem will start again.

A close relation of the familiar grey wolf is the red wolf, which once had the 'distinction' of being the world's most endangered mammal.

Now it is on the road to recovery thanks to being bred in captivity and then released into protected areas of the wild.

There *are* some bright spots, but wolves have a long way to go before they are safe. Most of all, their future depends on whether people change their attitudes towards wolves, and let them live in peace.

There are about 50 Mexican wolves left in the wild. They used to live not only in Mexico, but also in parts of the southern United States. They were relentlessly hunted by cattlemen who wanted to make sure that no wolf would ever attack their livestock.

Setting free a red wolf. It belongs to a project which is trying to save red wolves from extinction by breeding them in captivity and releasing them into the wild. They once lived in the south-eastern United States, but were wiped out by hunting and the destruction of their woodland homes.

Hounding the wolf

WOLVES USED TO BE the most wide-spread mammals in the world (apart from human beings) and were found throughout the woodlands of Europe, Asia and North America. Today, they have already died out in many places. Only in the remotest parts of Russia, Canada and Alaska do large numbers of them still live.

In ancient times, wolves and people both moved around in groups hunting animals to eat. The trouble started when people started making settlements. First, they cleared woodlands to make space for permanent dwellings, leaving wolves with less room to live in. Next, they began to keep farm animals. On finding all this penned-in food so easy to catch, the wolves helped themselves. Ever since then, the main bone of contention between wolves and people is that wolves eat animals that people are fattening up for themselves.

Wolves were branded as criminals and hunted down – indeed, not so long ago some convicts were let off their punishments if they killed a certain number of wolves.

Nowadays wolves are protected in some places, but in others they are still shot for stealing livestock.

Above: Wolves are friendly and affectionate with each other. Several families hunt, rest and play together – and all the adults in the pack help look after the pups.
Left: Does the story of Little Red Riding Hood draw a true picture of the wolf?

WILDSIDE WATCH

For wolves to survive we need to alter our attitude to them, something that can begin at home.
● We all know tales of wolves as 'baddies', but look for books that show more of the truth about these animals.
● Wolves and dogs are closely related. Find out about wolf social behaviour and compare it with a dog's. Look, for example, at a dog's body language, such as how it holds its tail and ears.
● Make other people aware of the bad press that wolves have received and put the story right.

Human predators

MAN IS THE MOST SUCCESSFUL HUNTER on Earth. He can't run like the leopard or the cheetah, and he doesn't have their teeth or claws. But he does have a big brain – and with it he can work out exactly how and when to attack. More important, he can make weapons.

Some of the first tools ever made were spears and clubs for killing animals, and some of the earliest pictures ever painted were of people hunting. Since prehistoric times, man has hunted in order to eat – but more advanced weapons like guns and traps have made it easy to kill many more creatures than are needed for food. The most famous animal made extinct by over-hunting is the dodo, which moved around slowly on the ground and was easy to kill. But others, including a duck which lives in trees, have nearly died out as a result of hunting.

Man the hunter

KEEPING ANIMALS SUCH AS SHEEP and pigs means that most of us don't need to go out and kill our own dinners. But large numbers of animals are hunted for sport.

People who take up this hobby are following in the footsteps of a long tradition. Centuries ago, some woodlands in Britain were saved from being chopped down so that the king could hunt deer whenever he felt like it. Today, there are woodlands in Europe and North America that are specially protected in order to provide people with places to go hunting; and deer are still some of the most commonly hunted animals.

In Europe, thousands of deer and wild boar are killed each year. Hunters say that if their numbers are not kept down, they would over-run the woodlands. Deer already do a lot of damage by stripping bark from trees and eating young shoots. One reason why their numbers are increasing is that man the hunter has got rid of animals like wolves and lynx that would normally kill and eat them.

Above: Some of the earliest cave paintings show people hunting animals.
Right: A family of wild boar forages in the forest. Baby boars lose their stripes when they are about six months old. A boar's natural lifespan is 15–20 years, but many have their lives cut short by hunters.

Preying on birds

THE ROBIN'S RED BREAST and tuneful song make it welcome in many woodlands and gardens, but in some countries it is hunted and eaten.

Every year thousands of robins and other small woodland birds are hunted down. Most of the killing occurs when they arrive back in Europe after spending the winter in Africa. Many are shot, but some are caught in nets or traps.

There are some laws to protect the birds, but hunters continue to kill them. Some people think the sport should be allowed to continue because it is traditional; the start of the hunting season is a time of festival and celebration. In the past, birds had a chance of escaping because guns weren't as effective as they are now. Today, automatic rifles seldom miss.

Above: By nesting in tree-hollows the wood duck escapes predators such as racoons. Its markings provide it with good camouflage in the woodland – but nothing has saved it from the gun.
Left: All over Europe, songbirds are shot and eaten. In one country, 1.5 million hunters kill between 100 and 250 million birds every year.

WILDSIDE
WATCH

There are arguments for and against hunting animals for meat and sport.
● Find out about both sides.
● Hold a debate about it in your class or school, with one group representing the hunters and another group the anti-hunters.
● Decide if you think any changes should be made to the laws which protect some animals from being hunted, but not others.
● Make sure the debate looks into different methods of hunting, which are hotly argued. Some animals are trapped, others shot, and some are still chased with dogs.

Hunting for fur

WITH ONLY A THIN covering of skin, human beings aren't very good at coping with cold weather. Many animals keep themselves warm and dry by having thick hair or fur – and we often wear their coats too. When wool is taken from sheep it is done without bloodshed and they soon grow more, but large numbers of other animals are killed to give us leather and fur.

We don't actually need to kill animals for their coats: there are plenty of other materials to make clothes from. But throughout history it has been fashionable to wear certain kinds of fur or skin, and demand for these has meant that people can make a lot of money selling them. Some animals have been hunted nearly to extinction just for the sake of fashion, and others suffer pain when they are caught alive in traps.

Beaver fur used to be the height of fashion. It is used to trim this hat and dress; the muff is also made from this warm fur.

Beavers

BEAVER-TAIL STEW used to appear on many a menu. Most beavers, however, were hunted not for their meat but for their fur. It was especially popular for hats because it is soft, warm and waterproof.

Beavers once ranged throughout Britain and Europe, but hunting wiped them out from many places as early as the fourteenth century. When Europeans first settled in North America they were delighted to find fresh supplies. The pattern was repeated, and the beaver disappeared from many areas. Luckily, beaver hats went out of fashion in time to save the last animals – although until quite recently the fur was used for the caps worn by soldiers of Britain's Royal Greenjackets regiment.

When it is in the water, the beaver is saved from getting soaked to the skin by its waterproof coat made of coarse, outer fur, with a soft, inner lining.

Tree teddy-bears

THE KOALA IS ONE OF Australia's most famous animals, but this tree-dwelling marsupial with the teddy-bear looks very nearly became extinct. The koala is often thought of as cuddly, and its soft coat proved to be its downfall. So many koalas were killed for their fur that they were wiped out completely from many areas by the beginning of this century. The last ones left were saved just in time, and today koalas are a strictly protected species.

Koalas are not hunted by other animals, so they have no need to be looking out for danger and have no need to run away. They spend their time sitting in eucalyptus trees eating leaves or just dozing. All the hunters had to do was point their guns and shoot. In one year alone almost two million koala skins were sold.

Thanks to today's protection, koalas are making a slow comeback, and some have been raised in special sanctuaries and returned to the wild. Even so, hunters still catch some koalas, and in one area the latest idea to stamp this out is to take finger-prints of every koala. If the police have a personal record of each animal, hunters might think twice before taking aim and firing.

The koala lives in trees, eats eucalyptus leaves, and sleeps 18 hours a day. At the beginning of this century, almost two million koalas were killed for their fur in one year alone.

Trading in pain

EVERY YEAR 50 million wild animals are killed for their fur. Many of these are woodland creatures such as sable, coyote, wolverine and lynx. A common way of catching them is to set a trap with sharp metal jaws. The jaws snap shut on the paw of the animal, and it may be stuck there in pain for several days before the hunter comes and kills it.

West Germany, the United States, and Japan are all major buyers of furs. In these countries the fur trade is big business. One full-length coyote coat, for example, costs £4500–£7000 ($8000–$14 000).

Paying the price: animals with fur coats are gassed, trapped and electrocuted just so that people can make a lot of money out of selling their skins.

WILDSIDE WATCH

Fur is made into all sorts of objects apart from hats and coats.
● **If you see rugs and ornaments made from endangered animals, tell an adult and they can report it. These are sometimes sold illegally as souvenirs.**
● **Find out about fur farming and decide what you think about it: some animals are specially reared to be killed for their fur.**

The disappearing butterfly

ANYONE OUT BUTTERFLY-SPOTTING might not choose to start their search in a shady wood. Open, sunny meadows seem more likely places to catch sight of those fluttering wings. But a good number of the world's 100,000 different butterflies are found only in woodlands. They are everywhere from ground level to the tops of trees, and in fact, some of the highest fliers are most often seen by bird-watchers with binoculars.

Butterflies know exactly what they are looking for. They live only in parts of a woodland where everything is just right for them, and the smallest disturbance can wipe them out.

Butterfly trees

IN THE WARMEST PARTS of North America, there are trees which no one is allowed to touch, let alone chop down. You may or may not be able to see why. It depends on when you look at them. Most of the time there is nothing special to see at all. But at the beginning of every winter, the trees suddenly become covered in monarch butterflies. Just one tree may be taken over by thousands, with whole branches completely hidden under thick clusters. No wonder they are known as 'butterfly trees'.

The butterflies appear as if from nowhere, but they have made long journeys to reach the trees. Most butterflies die in winter, but monarchs behave more like birds, and migrate to where it is warmer. They fly in swarms and rest in trees on the way, but do not stop until they get to Florida and California. There they settle on the same trees year after year, and go to sleep for winter. They leave in spring, but the trees are protected all year round so they are always ready to receive their winter guests.

Right: Thousands of monarch butterflies rest in one tree. Their bright colours help to save them from attack: if a bird eats one, it gets a nasty taste in its mouth because the monarch is poisonous – and the colours remind the bird not to try again.

Life cycle of the pearl-bordered fritillary
Unlike the monarch, most butterflies die in autumn – but they have laid the eggs which will become the next generation. All butterflies pass through four distinct stages. The length of each varies with different species, but the adult always emerges when the flowers are out. The pearl-bordered fritillary is one example of a woodland butterfly.

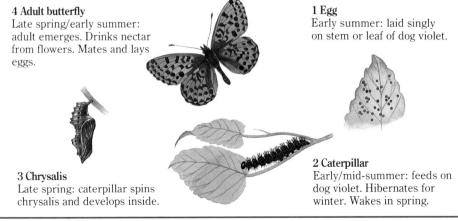

4 Adult butterfly
Late spring/early summer: adult emerges. Drinks nectar from flowers. Mates and lays eggs.

1 Egg
Early summer: laid singly on stem or leaf of dog violet.

3 Chrysalis
Late spring: caterpillar spins chrysalis and develops inside.

2 Caterpillar
Early/mid-summer: feeds on dog violet. Hibernates for winter. Wakes in spring.

Individual needs

CUTTING A PATH through a woodland need not lead to disaster. The path may bring people and dogs and noise, but some animals just keep well out of the way. Others, however, can find their whole lives ruined by the slightest changes.

Butterflies have very particular needs. Each type of butterfly lays its eggs on only one or two species of plant. These plants may be quite common, but the butterfly must choose certain individual plants. They may have to be just the right height, or at just the right stage of growth, or in just the right light. An ideal patch can be very easily spoiled. Add all the spoiled patches together, and you end up with some butterflies that are in serious danger of dying out altogether.

Poplar admiral
Lays eggs in poplar trees throughout Europe, but chooses only certain trees. Cutting down trees has completely wiped this butterfly out in some woodlands. The caterpillar eats poplar leaves and hibernates in winter.

Woodland brown
Found in woodland edges with grasses, on which it lays its eggs. It also seeks shade, so lives only in places with thick bushes and shrubs. Clearing these to make paths causes it to die out.

Chequered skipper
Extinct in England, but seen in some woodland glades of northern and central Europe. It feeds from flowers such as bugle and ground ivy, and disappears where these are destroyed.

WILDSIDE
WATCH

Keep an eye on your local butterflies.
● **Find out which ones are likely to be in your area, and which plants they lay their eggs on.**
● **Remember that eggs and caterpillars are much better off where they are than stuck inside a jar or matchbox.**
● **You can help butterflies by growing the plants they need. Why not convert a corner of a garden or wasteland into a butterfly patch?**

Australian dieback

IF YOU WALKED through the woodlands of south-western Australia you would see many animals and plants found nowhere else on Earth. You would walk between the tall, straight trunks of the jarrah trees, whose leathery leaves shade you from the hot sun; you would pick your way through brightly coloured flowers which light up the woodland floor; and you might even catch sight of the striped back of a squirrel-like creature called a numbat.

But you would also come across big, empty spaces. Many trees in these woodlands are dying from an incurable disease, and without the trees, everything else disappears. Luckily there are people who are trying to help the woodlands fight for survival.

Jarrahs at risk

EACH EVENING, before leaving for home, all the workers in the jarrah woodland clean their trucks. Every bit of mud picked up during the day is washed off. It's not the dirt that bothers them, but the fact that in the dirt live the tiny bits of fungus that are killing the trees. By hosing down their trucks the men make sure they don't spread the disease by carrying it to other parts of the woodland.

Following these strict rules of hygiene is one way in which people are trying to save the woodland. Another is to keep on searching for a cure. So far, scientists have learnt how the fungus spreads, but they haven't found out how to stop it.

It's just as well that something is being done to try and help the trees fight back, because it was probably people who caused the problem in the first place. Earlier this century, some plants from tropical countries were brought into Australia and grown right near the woodlands. The deadly fungus must have come with these plants.

As if one thing isn't enough, the trees are also being killed by caterpillars which chew their way through the leaves. *And* they are being cut down for their timber. These woodlands need all the help they can get!

Below right: The lush jarrah forest is home to a unique range of wildlife. Three-quarters of all the plant species do not grow anywhere else on earth. Right: The jarrah trees are one of the 500 species of eucalyptus. They can grow over 30 m (100 ft) tall, and live for hundreds of years. But now these trees are dying from a disease which rots their roots and makes them collapse.

Following strict rules of hygiene - even for their trucks - is one way in which the forest workers try to stop the disease from spreading.

Last hopes

IF THE TREES lose their fight to survive, many animals and plants will die out. Healthy parts of the woodlands are their last refuges. The honey possum, the woylie, and the chuditch are just three of the animals living here. The honey possum is a mouse-like creature small enough to sit on a flower and feed from it like an insect. The woylie looks like a mini-kangaroo and bounces along the woodland floor carrying bunches of grass in its tail to make itself a fresh bed under a bush. And with the looks and habits of a cat, the chuditch is a stealthy hunter of the night, a creature that is seldom seen.

These animals – and many more – seek food and shelter from the trees and other plants that fill the woodlands with huge flowers, spiky leaves and strange shapes. Nearly three-quarters of all the plant species growing in these woodlands are found nowhere else.

Above: The numbat was nearly wiped out in the last century when it was eaten by English foxes let loose in Australia by settlers who wanted to go fox-hunting. The jarrah forest is one of its last refuges.
Left: Like a bee, the honey possum feeds on the nectar of flowers. This tiny mammal is found only in south-western Australia.

WILDSIDE WATCH

You can help woodlands stay healthy by keeping a careful eye on them. Disease-causing fungi are too small to see, but bigger objects such as bags of rubbish or unwanted furniture are also bad for woods.
● If you spot any dumping, report it to whoever owns the wood.
● Organise regular litter collections in local woodlands or other natural places.
● Ask your local newspaper to take pictures of all the rubbish you collect.

The returning woodlands

AFTER A FIELD has been ploughed, bare earth is all there is to see. But you only have to look at a garden to find out that bare earth doesn't stay bare for long. Grasses and wildflowers soon appear – much to the dismay of gardeners who call them weeds and pull them up. Farmers, too, make sure no unwanted plants grow. However, if weeds were left to take over, there would, after some decades, be a full-scale woodland complete with trees, bushes, flowers and animals. Sooner or later, woodlands would cover almost any piece of land: all they need is to be left alone!

Trees as far as the eye can see – but only 60 years ago, this was fields of cows and corn! It's the Shenandoah Valley in Virginia in the United States, and is now a specially protected national park.

Shenandoah Valley

BOBCATS AND DEER, ravens and owls, and a whole host of other animals live amongst the tall, thick trees that lie across the Shenandoah Valley. The woodland is one of the wildest places in North America – but it hasn't always been like this. During the nineteenth century, there was not a deer or a bobcat or even a tree in sight here. Instead, there were farmhouses, cows, pigs, and fields of cabbages and corn. Settlers had cleared all the trees and farmed the land, but by the early part of this century the crops started to fail because the soil was worn out from so much planting. The government decided to give the area back to nature, so the people moved away and left the land to its own devices. It's still not a completely people-free zone, but visitors only come to look, then leave it be.

How the trees of Shenandoah came back

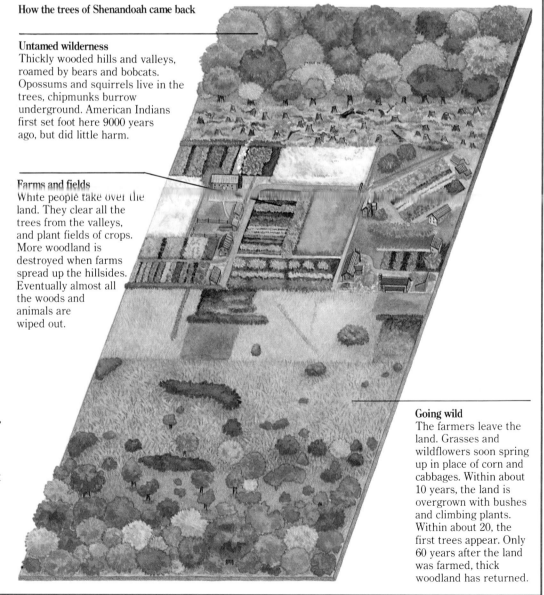

Untamed wilderness
Thickly wooded hills and valleys, roamed by bears and bobcats. Opossums and squirrels live in the trees, chipmunks burrow underground. American Indians first set foot here 9000 years ago, but did little harm.

Farms and fields
White people take over the land. They clear all the trees from the valleys, and plant fields of crops. More woodland is destroyed when farms spread up the hillsides. Eventually almost all the woods and animals are wiped out.

Going wild
The farmers leave the land. Grasses and wildflowers soon spring up in place of corn and cabbages. Within about 10 years, the land is overgrown with bushes and climbing plants. Within about 20, the first trees appear. Only 60 years after the land was farmed, thick woodland has returned.

Above: When is a wildflower a weed? Trillium now runs riot across the floor of the Shenandoah Valley in Virginia, in the United States – but when this land was farmed, all the wild plants were pulled up.

Left: The new woodland of the Shenandoah Valley is now officially described as 'wilderness' – and the bobcat gives its own stamp of approval by taking up residence here.

Below left: The copperhead snake tries not to be seen or heard, but its presence is a good sign. A healthy, natural woodland needs predators to help control the numbers of animals which eat the plants.

WILDSIDE
WATCH

● Go wild! Find out whether a corner of your local park, garden or school grounds can be left uncultivated.
● Keep a note of the plants that appear.
● Grow your own wood! Trees can be grown from seed.
● Choose species of trees that belong locally so that when the time comes to plant them out they will fit in with the naturally occurring ones.

Knock on wood

IT WOULD BE HARD to think up a bird better designed for living in a wood than a woodpecker. It has big, strong feet for climbing trees, claws that hold on tight, and a wedge-shaped tail to keep its balance. Its sharp beak is the perfect tool to open cracks in the bark, and its long tongue is just right for getting into them and licking up grubs and beetles. Its beak also hammers, drills and chisels, to make the holes in trees that woodpeckers live in. And all this banging doesn't even give the bird a headache, for its body has special shock-absorbers.

Woodlands would not be complete without woodpeckers, and no woodpeckers can live without woodlands. Cutting down trees robs a woodpecker of its whole world.

Wood preservers

WHENEVER SOMEONE CLAIMS to have seen or heard one particular woodpecker, all bird-watchers prick up their ears. It's the ivory-billed woodpecker, and it is on the very brink of extinction. Some say it has already died out, others say that a handful of birds are still alive in one or two woodlands. The destruction of their homes has caused the woodpeckers' plight, and even if some birds are still alive, their numbers are so low that they seem doomed to extinction.

Some other kinds of woodpecker are also in trouble, but at least they have the law on their side. Loggers and builders have been charged heavy fines for chopping down trees that rare woodpeckers were living in. In the latest attempt to reach a compromise, judges have allowed people to take some trees, providing they leave others for the birds. It looks as if this might suit everyone, because in return for board and lodging, the woodpeckers protect the loggers' trees by eating beetles that damage the wood.

Left: The red-cockaded woodpecker is already very rare. It will die out unless urgent action is taken to save the trees it lives in.

Right: Dead as a dodo? Destruction of its woodland home has caused the extinction of the ivory-billed woodpecker in North America. A few birds *may* still be alive in Cuba.

Woodpeckers bite back

IN SOME PLACES where trees have been chopped down, woodpeckers have turned their beaks on telegraph poles. They drilled so many holes that the poles had to be replaced. People tried stopping them by coating poles with chemicals, but the woodpeckers weren't put off. Then the poles were wrapped in wire and plastic, but the woodpeckers pecked their way through. Finally, toy snakes were stuck to poles to make the woodpeckers think they were in danger of being eaten, but the birds weren't fooled.

So far, the woodpeckers have got the better of people, but all they're doing is looking for a place to live and something to eat. What they really need is their trees back.

Left: Making nest-holes in telegraph poles is one way of getting the message across: woodpeckers need trees!

A home from home?

PUTTING A SELECTION of scraps on a bird table is one way of doing birds a good turn – but woodpeckers don't always show their appreciation. Some people have discovered their tables collapsed on the ground because a woodpecker has pecked through the central post! Bags of peanuts are also at the mercy of woodpecker beaks, and get ripped up with gusto. The best way of feeding a woodpecker is to offer it something it is more used to. Holes made in an old log and filled with fat and seeds should do the trick.

Woodpeckers that take up residence in bird boxes usually improve their homes by pecking at entrance holes to make them bigger. They are not often found using boxes, but plenty of other woodland birds whose homes are demolished are only too glad of them.

Bird boxes
Putting up bird boxes saves lives. Many birds nest in holes in trees, so cutting down trees leaves them homeless. The boxes are artificial tree-holes.

WILDSIDE WATCH

Make sure woodpeckers have woods to live in.
● **If there are woods near you, join any conservation groups that aim to make sure they will not be destroyed.**
● **If you put food out for woodpeckers and other birds, take your responsibilities seriously and be sure to feed them every day. They will soon come to rely on you.**
● **Put out a shallow bowl of warm water when the ground is frozen – many birds die in winter because they can't find any water.**

Defending bats

A BAT'S LIST of creature comforts includes a good home, a well-balanced diet, and huge helpings of peace and quiet. Woodlands provide plenty of all four. For 50 million years, bats have been living in hollow trees, eating insects, and sleeping. But about five million years ago a major disturbance took place: the first people appeared on Earth. Ever since then we've been demolishing their homes, destroying their food-supply, and even killing them. At last we're waking up to the fact that bats need help – but if we're not quick about it their days on Earth are numbered.

Fact or fiction?

NO, THEY DON'T get tangled in your hair, no, they don't go around sinking their teeth into people's necks, and no, they're not blind! Bats are harmless and shy and much misunderstood. True, they have some rather individual habits – like hanging upside down by their feet for hours on end, or eating meals in the middle of the night – but real bats bear very little resemblance to those evil fiends of horror stories.

In fact, bats are quite like people. They're mammals like us, they live in families, and they take good care of their children. It's high time we laid the story of Dracula to rest and got to know real bats better.

Nights on the town

WITH ALL THE BRIGHT LIGHTS and the hustle and bustle, a city street is the last place you would expect to find an animal that likes a quiet life. But so many woodlands have been destroyed that bats are forced to take up residence in urban areas. There they make do with living in the space inside roofs, although sometimes they find they have flown into a death-trap. Some people dislike these harmless lodgers, and simply kill them, or else the bats get poisoned by chemicals put on roof beams to preserve the wood.

Food also poses problems, for insects can be scarce in built-up areas. But some insects are attracted to lights at night, so the bats hang round city lampposts in the hope that they may be able to catch a snack.

Right: Destroying woodlands renders many bats homeless. This Bechstein's bat is forced to seek board and lodging in a garden shed. It is just one of many species which are now becoming very rare.

Left: Bats have been thought to be evil and scaring for a very long time. In pictures, the Devil often has bat wings.
Above: This cartoon makes fun of the bad image bats have, in order to help us think better of them. The Bat Conservation Trust uses it in campaigns to persuade people to be kind to bats.

Attract a bat

IF YOU HAVE BATS in your attic you should consider yourself highly honoured. Bats are very choosy where they live, and actually prefer modern buildings without dust or cobwebs!

Nothing can replace an old, hollow tree, but with a large number of these now gone, the next best thing might be a bat box. Having tried lots of shapes and sizes, bat experts have come up with the right kind of box – but you must think carefully about its position. Bats like to be out of the wind, and in the sun, but in a place that is not too hot.

These are the different components needed to build a standard bat box.

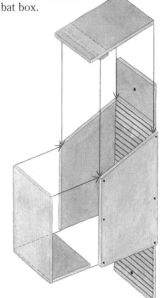

Side view of bat box

Bats enter through a gap in the base.

One important way of helping bats is to provide them with somewhere to live. Here, a bat box is being fixed in a tree. It must be very carefully placed, out of the wind but unobstructed by branches.

WILDSIDE
WATCH

Across the world there are nearly 1000 species of bat, some of which are amongst the most seriously threatened of mammals.
● Find out which species of bat belong where you live, and whether they are threatened.
● If you know of bats living in roofs or boxes, do not disturb them because they may then leave their home and not come back.
● If you know of anyone having a new roof installed ask them to check and make sure that any chemicals being used are safe for bats.

Handle with care

WHENEVER ANYONE talks about extinction, the dodo soon pops up. Everyone knows that dodos were flightless birds that didn't run out of the way when men shot at them – and that consequently the men got lots of meat and all the dodos died out. Now, 200 years later, we're pushing more and more animals and plants towards extinction.

But there's another chapter to the dodo story. It turns out that killing the birds caused a type of tree to die out too, because its seeds can't grow unless they've been eaten by a dodo and come out the other end. Which just goes to show that we can't keep taking pieces out of the natural world and expect what's left to carry on as if nothing has happened.

The exciting thing is that we're still learning how everything fits together in all the different woodlands of the world. But urgent action is needed to make sure we don't lose any more pieces.

LOCATION
Ancient oak trees, central Europe
THREATENED SPECIES
Longhorn beetle
TOTAL POPULATION
Unknown. Once widely distributed in Europe. Now extinct in some countries. Very rare everywhere.
THREATS
Killed for being a pest, felling of old oaks

The beetle larvae burrow into the tree, making finger-wide tunnels. The tree is unharmed, and goes on growing with them inside it. But the wood can't be used for timber, so foresters have systematically killed all the beetles they can find, and even cut down trees to get at the beetles. Now, some of the last beetles are protected in parts of Austria, Czechoslovakia and Poland.

LOCATION
Central Queensland, Australia
THREATENED SPECIES
Bridled nailtail wallaby
TOTAL POPULATION
Once thought to be extinct. One small population discovered in 1973.
THREATS
Destruction of habitat, eaten by introduced foxes

Herds of cows and sheep are now where the wallabies once lived. Kilometres of grassy woodlands and thickets have been turned into open fields. Some wallabies died out when the farm animals ate all the plants that they depend on. Other wallabies were killed when the destruction of the woodlands left them with nowhere to hide from the foxes and dogs which eat them.

LOCATION
Delmarva Peninsula, Maryland, USA
THREATENED SPECIES
Delmarva fox squirrel
TOTAL POPULATION
Probably under 1000.
THREATS
Woodland clearance for farming and house building

Ancient woodland bordering streams is the home of the fox squirrel, which searches for nuts at the foot of trees such as hickory, beech, and loblolly pine. Felling trees to make way for farms and houses has caused its extinction in most of the north-eastern United States. A special Fox Squirrel Recovery Team is trying to save the last survivors.

LOCATION
Tanzania, Africa
THREATENED SPECIES
African violet
TOTAL POPULATION
Now grows only in Uzungwa forest.
THREATS
Woodland clearance for farming

Within the last 50 years, the African violet has become one of the commonest and most popular house-plants. But while thousands are grown in pots, their wild counterparts are being wiped out. The violet grows only in Tanzania, and is now found in just one woodland there. Clearing the woodland to make space for crops and farm animals is bringing about its extinction.

WILDSIDE WATCH

Scientists estimate that we will soon be making one species extinct every single day. Here's how you can help to save woodlands and their wildlife.
● Find out about the work of different conservation organisations.
● Get involved with some of their campaigns.
● Remember that joining a conservation group can get you in on the action close to home, *and* keep you up to date with what's going on worldwide.

Save the woodlands

THERE ARE NO two ways about it: woodlands need your help! And they need it *now*. Lots of people are already taking action to save the trees and their wildlife, but just think what a difference it would make if we all joined in. You don't need to be an expert, or even to get your hands dirty! There are 101 ways you can help – so just choose what you'd like to do. It could be anything from learning more about woodlands and showing people how important they are, to joining campaigns which protect natural places near where you live. And *that* could be a whole woodland or a few trees along a city street. Remember that one tree can be a nature reserve in its own right – and by keeping an eye on it, you could save it. Plenty of trees are destroyed because no one speaks up for them. So get going today, and turn yourself into a woodland watchdog!

Above: Get back to nature! There are lots of ways you can spend some time in the great outdoors – and lend a hand to wildlife into the bargain. Here, brushwood is being piled into heaps for small birds to nest in, and mammals such as voles and shrews to hide under.

Left: Many countries have special days when everyone takes action to help the planet. These people are in Rock State Park, Arizona, to celebrate North America's Earth Day. Planting trees is one of the best ways of giving the Earth something back for all we take from it.

Below: A good first step towards taking care of a woodland is to get to know it. Woods are easy to get to know if you treat them politely! Keep your voice down, watch where you tread, and open your eyes and ears.

Useful addresses

Here is a list of useful organisations for you to contact. It is a good idea to send a stamped, self-addressed envelope with your request for information.

WATCH Clubs
c/o The Royal Society for Nature Conservation (RSNC)
The Green
Witham Park
Waterside South
Lincoln LN5 7JR
Young people's conservation group. Members take part in national and local activities, such as testing for acid rain and creating nature reserves.

Earth Action
c/o Friends of the Earth
26–28 Underwood Street
London N1 7JQ
Young people's organisation which campaigns to protect the environment. Local branches organise recycling schemes and conservation projects in their own neighbourhoods.

World Wide Fund for Nature (WWF)
Panda House
Weyside Park
Godalming
Surrey GU7 1XR
Runs international campaigns to save endangered animals and their habitats.

British Trust for Conservation Volunteers (BTCV)
36 St Mary's Street
Wallingford
Oxford OX10 0EU
Organises volunteers to carry out conservation work in their local area. Also runs conservation working-holidays.

The Woodland Trust
Autumn Park
Dysart Road
Grantham
Lincs NG31 6LL
Conserves woodlands, and plants trees. Runs projects which involve people in looking after their local woodlands.

The Tree Council
35 Belgrave Square
London SW1X 8QN
Protects and plants trees. Appoints volunteer tree wardens to look after local woodlands. Organises tree-planting projects.

Young Ornithologists' Club (YOC)
c/o The Royal Society for the Protection of Birds
The Lodge
Sandy
Beds SG19 2DL
Young people's organisation which campaigns to protect birds.

The Hawk and Owl Trust
c/o The London Zoological Society
Regents Park
London NW1 4RY
Aims to protect all birds of prey. Members can take part in local surveys and conservation projects.

The Young Batworkers Club
c/o The Conservation Foundation
1 Kensington Gore
London SW7 2AR
Campaigns for the protection of all bats. Batworkers carry out fieldwork and conservation projects.

Lynx
P.O. Box 300, Nottingham NG1 5HN
Campaigns to stop all trade in animal fur.

Index

Picture credits (key: l – left, r – right, t – top, c – centre, b – bottom, tl – top left, tr – top right, bl – bottom left, br – bottom right)
Ardea pages 5 (br), 10 (br, Å. Lindau), 25 (b, R. Smith), 36 (t, J. van Gruisen), 39 (b, R. Smith), 46 (l, K. Fink), 47 (l), 60 (H. & J. Beste) and 61 (b, K. Fink); **Auscape** pages 10 (t, E. Beaton), 49 (l, C. A. Henley) and 52–3 (J.-P. Ferrero); **Jim Brandenburg** pages 44–5; **Bridgeman Art Library/Private Collection** ('Life on the Prairie - the Buffalo Hunt', 1862, by Currier & Ives) page 9; **British Museum/Natural History** page 56 (l); **C. A. Callahan** page 33 (r, from 'On-site methods for assessing chemical impact on the soil environment using earthworms', by C. A. Callahan, C. A. Menzie, D. E. Burmaster, D. C. Wilborn, T. Ernst, pub. in 'Environmental Toxicology & Chemistry', vol. 10, no. 6, 16 May 1991); **Bruce Coleman** pages 4 (c, H. Reinhard), 14 (J. Foott), 23 (t, J. Burton), 25 (t, H. Reinhard), 27 (t & b, G. Cubitt), 32 (b, M. Viard), 35 (J. Foott), 38–9 (A. Purcell), 40 (l, H. Reinhard), 43 (b, K. Wothe), 46 (r, H. Reinhard), 47 (r, S. Nielsen), 58–9 (H. Reinhard) and 60–1 (H. Rivarola); **DRK Photo** pages 37 (l, Johnny Johnson) and 62 (T. Bean); **Mary Evans Picture Library** pages 44 (r) and 58 (l); **Explorer** page 49 (r, C. Lenars); **Jennifer Fry** page 24 (l); **Hanna-Barbera Productions Inc.** © 1991 page 37 (r); **Holt Studios** page 19 (t); **Eric & David Hosking** pages 8–9 and 23 (b, J. Hawkins); **Jacana** page 36 (b, J. M. Labat); **Frank Lane** pages 5 (t, S. McCutcheon), 10 (bl, H. Hautala), 16 (S. Maslowski), 26 (r, D. Grewcock), 29 (l, B. S. Turner), 31 (R. Tidman), 48 (b, M. Newman), 56–7 (A. R. Hamblin), 59 (r, R. Tidman) and 63 (b, C. Newton); **Network** page 32 (t, C. Pillitz); **Peter Newark's Historical Pictures** page 48 (t); **NHPA** page 4 (t, J. Shaw; b, D. Woodfall), 5 (c, S. Krasemann), 24 (r, D. Woodfall), 39 (t, S. Krasemann), 42 (E. Soder), 43 (tl, M. Danegger), 44 (c, S. Krasemann) and 52 (br, ANT/J. Taylor); **Oxford Scientific Films** pages 18–19 (O. Newman), 19 (b, T. Heathcote), 21 (b, P. Henry; r, T. Heathcote), 33 (l, D. Thompson), 40 (r, M. Leach) and 52 (t & b, B. Wells); **Photo Researchers** pages 11 (R. Lynn), 25 (l, G. C. Kelley), 41 (T. Davis), 44 (l, G. C. Kelley), 54 and 55 (tl, L. L. Rue; tr, J. Lepore; b, National Audubon Society/A. E. Staffan); **Planet Earth Pictures** pages 4 (bl, N. Downer), 20 (M. Mattock), 21 (l, C. Read), 26 (l, D. Klees/Worldview), 30 (E. Neal) and 50–1 (K. Lucas); **Michael Quinton** pages 14–15 and 15 (t & b); **RSPB** pages 5 (bl, C. H. Gomersall), 43 (b, C. H. Gomersall) and 63 (t, Ash); **Survival Anglia** pages 28–9 (T. & L. Bomford), 29 (r, M. Wilding) and 61 (r, J. Foott); **Westpics** page 52 (bl, E. Collis); **Windsor Castle, Royal Library** © **1990 Her Majesty the Queen** page 56 (r); **David Woodfall** page 12.
Illustrators Alan Male, Shane Marsh, David Moore, Jane Pickering, Sebastian Quigley, Phil Weare, David Webb, (Linden Artists). Helen Senior.